T0156924

A Prayer Warrior After God's Own Heart

—— *An Easy Read for All People* ——

Apostle Nenkawah Barnabas Gbeintor

WESTBOW
PRESS®
A DIVISION OF THOMAS NELSON
& ZONDERVAN

Copyright © 2017 Apostle Nenkawah Barnabas Gbeintor.

All rights reserved. No part of this book may be used or reproduced by any means, graphic, electronic, or mechanical, including photocopying, recording, taping or by any information storage retrieval system without the written permission of the author except in the case of brief quotations embodied in critical articles and reviews.

This book is a work of non-fiction. Unless otherwise noted, the author and the publisher make no explicit guarantees as to the accuracy of the information contained in this book and in some cases, names of people and places have been altered to protect their privacy.

Scripture taken from the King James Version of the Bible.

WestBow Press books may be ordered through booksellers or by contacting:

WestBow Press
A Division of Thomas Nelson & Zondervan
1663 Liberty Drive
Bloomington, IN 47403
www.westbowpress.com
1 (866) 928-1240

Because of the dynamic nature of the Internet, any web addresses or links contained in this book may have changed since publication and may no longer be valid. The views expressed in this work are solely those of the author and do not necessarily reflect the views of the publisher, and the publisher hereby disclaims any responsibility for them.

Any people depicted in stock imagery provided by Thinkstock are models, and such images are being used for illustrative purposes only.
Certain stock imagery © Thinkstock.

ISBN: 978-1-9736-0901-8 (sc)
ISBN: 978-1-9736-0900-1 (e)

Print information available on the last page.

WestBow Press rev. date: 12/13/2017

Contents

Introduction

People always say that knowledge is power, but I believe knowledge is potential power while wisdom makes the power a reality. Understanding is knowing what to do, while wisdom is knowing how to do it. Knowing the word of God does not guarantee victory. A soldier on the battlefield can have the best sword ever made and may know everything about it such as the type of steel used to make it, the length, weight and other statistics, but if he doesn't know how to lift it up towards the enemy, hold it in the proper stance and know how to wield it in combat, he will die against an enemy who has inferior weapons but knows how to use them.

Knowing that we need to pray, and even how to pray, in the sense that prayer is talking to God, is potential knowledge. Learning how to use the word of God in our prayers is the wisdom that this book will offer to its readers and enable us to become a master swordsman. With the teachings in this book, you will not just become just another piece of cannon fodder on the battlefield; a private fresh out of boot camp with no real combat experience, but a five-star general in the spirit world.

While we are never called to start a fight (Romans 12:18), if someone is fighting you, do not back down or surrender; instead finish the fight. The bible calls our enemy "the adversary" (1 Peter 5:8). Your adversary is someone who looks for an occasion to steal from you, kill you, or destroy you. Your adversary has no mercy and shows no pity or remorse towards you. He and his minions are irrational in their hatred for you. This describes our enemy, the devil, pretty well, and this description sticks to his nature like Gorilla Glue!

When the devil walks to and fro, and up and down in the earth, he knows the truth. In fact, the bible says he is "wiser than Daniel" (Ezekiel 28:3). When he looks at you, he is searching to see if you know the truth. In Mark 4:3-20, Jesus told a parable of a person who scattered seed around, then likened the results of his sowing to different kinds of people. He said the first seeds fell by the wayside, never taking root, while other seeds represent people who allow their lifestyle and things of the world to choke it off.

I encourage you not to let the Word of God sown in your hearts lay by the wayside where the fowls of the air come by and eat it, or allow the weeds to choke it off and displace it. The reason Satan comes immediately to take the word sowed in our hearts is because he knows the potential power of the word of God once it Is received by a child of God. He fears the seed taking root and achieving its potential by enabling a Christian to become a Prayer Warrior.

The word of God is like a receipt. We need to keep it so that it can be presented at all times whenever needed. The word of God is for our profit; therefore, Satan comes immediately to try and steal it as soon as it's sowed. This is the time to make sure he does not succeed, instead allow our passion to be turned into action by God's grace.

Have you lost your faith to pray in the storm?

Have you arrived at a point in your life where you have lost your desire to pray? At one time, you may have enjoyed spending time talking to God, but now it seems like a chore and something to be avoided. This feeling especially comes during mental attacks from Satan's mind games. This discouragement is because you and many others are lacking substance in your prayer life, and because of this, your prayers ring hollow and seem to have no purpose, resulting in your no longer having a desire to pray. The truth is, you do not even know how or what to pray for when you do decide to pray. As soon as you make up your mind to pray, your eyes start to close and sleep overcomes you. Sometimes, your phone rings, someone knocks on the door, or some other distraction makes it impossible for you to pray. This is not just a coincidence or an accident, it is by design.

The devil does not want you to have a quality prayer life, and until you attend to the seriousness of this attack upon your spiritual life, your life will continue to function like a rocking chair; moving but not going anywhere. You do know that you are in a spiritual war right? You might not see Satan physically trying to hinder you from praying, just as Elisha's servant could not see the spiritual war raging around him (2 Kings 6:15-17), but the outcome can be clearly seen and felt by you.

Yes, I said it. Your prayer life is weak, and every day Satan taunts you in your mind, reminding you of how weak it is. While this is true, do not be discouraged, because God said He will never leave you, nor forsake you."

The truth is, the devil doesn't just hate you, but all those who desire a better relationship with Jesus Christ and want to progress spiritually in all godliness. He hates the image of God in you, your happiness, victory, joy, families, future, and most especially, God's divine purpose for your life on earth. He is angry that you took his place as the apple of God's eye. Satan no longer has his lofty position in Heaven. He is now on death row because he has been judged.

You are not alone in this fight. You can obtain victory in this battle as you increase your ability to pray more effectively. Just as a rifle instructor can take a raw recruit and make him into an expert marksman if he is willing to listen and apply the knowledge, this book will make sure that you learn how to become an effective prayer warrior.

Let me take a moment to enlighten each of us who are called to be a prayer warrior; there are three persons in you:

1. The person your friends think you are.
2. The person you want to become.
3. The person you truly are; this is what God created you to be.

You are a prayer warrior, a person called, and chosen by God to pray effectively while using the word of God in this wicked generation.

Deep down, you know this is true because it is your heart's desire. Satan also knows this because he has been trying to stop you from praying effectively for a long time. I only have good news for you from this point forward; God has heard your cry, and His Precious Holy spirit has driven me to help manifest your heart's desire by writing this book to teach you how to become a prayer warrior. This is your request being granted by your Heavenly Father.

Once you start reading this book and applying the teaching, your prayer life will flourish like a palm tree planted by the rivers of water. Your life will be lifted to new heights. You will be operating on the top level spiritually, and you will be the head in every area of your life, instead of the tail; in Jesus' name. Prayer moves mountains, and an active prayer warrior is the number one threat to the devil. People will call you blessed because of your ability to stand in the gap and pray concerning all things. God is looking for such a person as He was in Ezekiel 22:30. "I searched for a man or woman among them who would build up the wall and stand in the gap before Me for the land, so that I would not destroy it, but I found no one." How wonderful it is that you are stepping up to read this book and being willing to learn how to become a prayer warrior who will stand in the gap for this land, which has such an urgent need.

In this book, you will see prayer points that contain recommended prayers each day or when going through some particular trial or heartache. It is vital that you understand that the actual words are intended to be more of an example rather than something you should pray by rote like Buddhist monks reciting a prayer wheel. In the military, while all go through the same training, it is also understood that every solider has their own personality and is expected to use the unique perspective they bring to the battle.

Part of this personality difference is in the way we communicate. Some people are more outgoing and laid back while other people speak in a more formal way. Some like cutting up in a conversational style while others feel they have to choose every word carefully. God made you in a special way to communicate the way you do. When you pray, do not try to be someone you are not. Let your unique conversational style be reflected in your prayer life. This will make you authentic rather than trying to be someone you are not. Also, it shows that you know you are talking to a real person rather than just reciting words in a script. God wants to carry on a conversation with you, based on your personality, not that of someone else. Please, do not deprive God of that privilege.

Preparations for Prayer

Confess your sins and ask for forgiveness

When preparing to have a prayer session, it is extremely important to confess your sins before the Lord. This is not something that should only be done prior to praying; instead you should do it whenever you become aware of a sin you may have committed. The old saying goes, "keep short accounts with God." We serve a Holy God who does not hear sinners. (John 9:31). David said, "If I regard iniquity in my heart, the Lord will not hear me" (Psalm 66:18). The word says in Romans 3:23, "For all have sinned and come short of the glory of God." The good news is that we have eternal victory through the blood of Jesus Christ. Taking time to confess and ask God to cleanse us of our daily sins displays our level of humility before the Almighty. He resists the pride, but gives grace to the humble (James 4:6). "If we say that we have no sin, we deceive ourselves, and the truth is not in us. If we confess our sins, He is faithful and just to forgive us our sins, and to cleanse us from all unrighteousness" (1 John 1:8-10).

Confessing is basically saying the same thing God is saying concerning us, that we are all sinners in His sight, period! The funny things is, this shouldn't be all that difficult because all we're doing is telling him something he already knows. I want to encourage you to not worry about hurting the Lord's feeling when confessing before Him because the bible tells us in Psalm 103:14 that "He knows our frame, and He remembers that we are dust." Many people complain in frustration, asking why their prayers are not answered. The truth is, God's hand is not shortened that it cannot save, neither is His ear heavy, that it cannot hear. But our iniquities have separated us from Him, and our sins have hid His face from us so he will not hear us. This is the reason you and I must invest the time to acknowledge our sins before the Lord prior to seeking Him in prayer.

"Blessed are they whose inequities are forgiven, and whose sins are covered. Blessed is the man to whom the Lord will not consider his sin." (Romans 4:7-8).

Give God thanks

Enter into His gates with thanksgiving. (Psalm 100:4)

I urge you to take time and thank the Lord for all His goodness in all He continues to do for you. Just raise your hands in the air and begin to thank Him, saying something like, "O Lord I thank you, I thank you for my day, even though the devil meant evil for me today. I thank you because you turned it around for my good. I thank you Lord for bringing my children home safely from school, thank you for providing food and water each and every day. Thank you for good health because I am not lying in the hospital. I thank you for my job, shelter, and a vehicle which takes me to and fro safely every day. Thank you for what you have done, and especially for what I know you are doing on my behalf right now. I thank you for this breath of life which I am experiencing, I thank you Lord because you are so good to me, and all that concerns my life.

Give God Praise Before Praying

Enter into His courts with praise. (Psalm 100:4)

Just because you have entered His gates with thanksgiving does not guarantee that you will see the King of Kings! You must enter into His courts with praise. Queen Esther only obtained favor after she entered into the king's court (Esther 5:2). When we pray, angels come; but when we start praising God in the beauty of His holiness, the King becomes immediately attentive and focuses in on our position. Praising the Lord prior to praying will invite you into the King's court where you get immediate attention by the King. Why? Because God inhabits the praises of His people! (Psalm 22:3)

The bible says in Acts 16:25, "and at midnight Paul and Silas prayed, and sang Praises unto God." Verse 26 tells us that immediately all the doors were opened and everybody's chains fell off. Praise the mighty name of Jesus! I see some chains being broken, unfastened, and loosed in your lives from your praising in the name of Jesus Christ. I encourage you to put on your garment of praise before entering your prayer section.

Pray with Faith

Hebrews 11:1 defines faith as "being sure of what we hope for and certain of what we do not see." I say to you, my brothers and sisters in Christ, there is no need to waste your precious time praying if you doubt the possibilities of what you are praying about. James 1:6-7 sums it up a little better for us. "But let him or her ask in faith without doubting, for he or she who doubts is like the surf of the seas, driven and tossed by the wind. For that person should not expect to receive anything from the Lord."

The only reason you and I pray is due to our faith, so why not keep that same attitude during your prayer session. Faith tells me that God is working all things out for my good, and that whatever I am praying for has already been accomplished by God.

Let me remind you that we are children of the promise which is through the faith of our father Abraham. "So then they which be of faith are blessed with faithful Abraham" (Galatians 3:9). Jesus teaches us in Mark 11:23-24 that, "Truly I say to you, whoever says to this mountain, Be taken up and cast into the sea, and does not doubt in his or her heart, but believes that what he or she says is going to happen, it will be granted them. Therefore I say to you, all things for which you pray, and ask, believe that you have received them, and they will be granted unto you." God only operates in our lives based on our faith. I would never limit anyone from achieving greater things, all we need is faith the size of a mustard seed to move our mountains.

Pray Consistently and Persistently

God is a God of time. We see in Ecclesiastes 3:1 that there is a purpose for everything under the sun. Just because it is not your time and season of manifestation does not mean you should tire and stop praying to God. God told Abraham in Genesis 17:21 that His wife was going to bear him a child at the appointed time.

This appointed time took place in Genesis 21:2, when the Lord visited Sarah just as He had said, and Sarah conceived a child for Abraham in her old age. Jesus also knew divine timing. We see in John 2:4 when His mother mentioned to him that the people needed wine, Jesus answered "mine hour is not yet come." In John 7:6, Jesus replied to His disciples that His time had not yet fully come. Then, in John 19:30, after the soldiers put vinegar to his mouth, Jesus said, "It is finished."

The greatest frustration we face today among both believers and unbelievers is their eagerness in expecting things to happen on their timetable.

The bible comforts us in Galatians 6:9, "let us not be weary in well doing, for at the proper time, or season we will reap a harvest if we faint not, or give up." To be honest with you, if you are alive and reading this book, then please take a moment to thank God for the time you have right now! Say to yourself, "I am blessed with the gift of life. In Jesus' name. Amen.

The reality of life is that sometimes we need God to move upon over lives in a special way but God also needs us to wait on Him in prayer in a special way! This proves that love is a two-way street!

Jesus urges us in Luke 18:1, "Then Jesus told his disciples a parable to show them that they should always pray and not give up." Sometimes, we want to give up in frustration. When this happens, and it will, continue to pray, for God is watching to see how persistent your heart is before Him.

Persistent- existing for a long period of time or longer than usual or continuously.

God is watching to see how patient and determined we are in our prayer life. This kind of person prays without ceasing or fainting, not because of what God can do for them, but simply because there is fullness of joy in the Lord's presence.

Your persistence in prayer lets God know that you know that He is able to deliver you from the lion's den and make your iron float on top of the water. That's a Mighty Prayer Warrior!

Jesus describes such a person in Luke 18:2-8. The bible tells us there was an unrighteous judge in a city who did not fear God, nor respect any man. One day a widow came to visit him, requesting legal protection from her adversary. At first, the unrighteous judge was unwilling to help her, but she kept asking over and over again for him to protect her. Finally, he was so overwhelmed by her petitions that he said to himself, even though I do not fear God, nor do I fear man, I will give her legal protection because I am tired of hearing her coming and bothering me every day.

Here is a great revelation for your spirit; God wants you to wear Him out with your prayers. When we get tired, God says "keep the prayers coming my children!" Jesus told his disciples that if this unrighteous judge was willing to change his mind and bestow blessings on this widow due to her persistency, how much more would God do to us, his children, whom he loves. This widow was a persistent prayer warrior who knew how to fight the devil and get blessings from God. Keep praying my brothers, and sisters, be patient for our God makes all things beautiful in his own time.

End All Prayers in the Name of Jesus

Any prayer that is not in the name of Jesus is a wasted prayer. The reason is, Jesus gives us the authority to have our prayers answered. Being fully God and fully man, Jesus is our mediator (Colossians 1:15-19)! He is the image of the invisible God, the firstborn of every creature. By Jesus all things were created that are in heaven and earth, both visible, and invisible, whether they be thrones, or dominions, or principalities, or power. All things were created by Jesus, and for Jesus Christ. He is before all things, and by Him all things consist, or are held together. For God was pleased to have all His fullness dwell in His Son Jesus Christ.

At the name of Jesus, every knee shall one day bow, of things in heaven, and things in the earth, and things under the earth. There will come a time when everyone you have witnessed to will acknowledge the truth of the gospel you gave them. The devil will also bow one day, but it will be too late for them. Because of all this power given to Jesus by the Father, there is no other name under heaven by which our prayers can be answered beside the name of Jesus Christ. Ending your prayers in the name of Jesus secures it.

Jesus said in John 14:14, "If you ask anything in my name, I will do it."

Pray the Word of God Back to God

The reason for writing this book is to teach people things the Lord taught me in the early days of my ministry regarding prayer; especially now when there is such an urgent need in our nation for prayer warriors to rise to the occasion. I have always believed in the power of excellence, even when I was not familiar with the word while growing up. I might not be a rich man with the ability to wear new clothes every day, but the clothes I do have, I take to the dry cleaners!

Solomon, the wisest man who ever lived, tells us, "Whatsoever thy hand findeth to do, do it with thy might; for there is no work, nor device, nor knowledge, nor wisdom, in the grave, whither thou goest" (Ecclesiastes 9:10). This is the reason God inspired me to write a book on praying His word back to Him, and to inspire this generation to understand the power this kind of prayer can bring into their lives. This book will be used for this generation, and the generations to come by His people in every nation. God has shown me that using His words in our daily prayers is the best and most effective way of praying to Him. One reason is that the word of God is so powerful that God Himself submits to it. "I will worship toward thy holy temple, and praise thy name for thy lovingkindness and for thy truth: **for thou hast magnified thy word above all thy name**" (Psalm 138:2). Because God has elevated the word of God above his name, it only makes sense to quote scripture back to him and point out what he said. Then, in a reverential way, tell God you are going to hold him accountable for what he wrote.

I did not know I was to be a prayer warrior until two years after the Lord called me into the ministry. When the Lord called me, He led to me to a variety of scriptures. The one scripture which inspired and clarified my calling is Jeremiah 15:16. "Thy words were found, and I did eat them: and thy word was unto me the joy and rejoicing of mine heart, for I am called by thy name, O Lord of hosts."

This scripture spoke to my soul when I first glimpsed it, so immediately the Holy Spirit instructed me to eat it, and I did. To become this kind of prayer warrior, you must delight in God's word. Being filled with the words of life makes my prayer life so much more powerful because the only thing that comes out when I am praying is the word of God, and this is the language that God speaks and understands. The Lord said to me, "My son, if you or anyone wants to see how fast I move, they must learn to pray my words back to Me."

The Lord said to me that he knows there are many other ways to pray based on the wide variety of prayer books written, and He is not discrediting these various methods, but "My people are not praying effectively because they are not listening to the Holy spirit; and if they were, they would know what my plans were for their lives." The Lord said to me that His people have forgotten the most important ability of His Holy Spirit, as written in (John 16:15), where Jesus said, "Everything that the Father has is mine." That is what I meant when I said that the Spirit will take things that are mine and will reveal, declare, disclose, and transmit them to you. You see, my spirit is not a translator, but a transmitter.

"I have given my people the ability to receive heavenly information concerning my will on earth, but they have strayed away from my heart's desire because they refused to listen to the guidance of my Holy Spirit due to a lack of prayer." The Lord encouraged me to not just teach His people how to pray, but to teach them to pray using His word. This is the kind of prayer that brings forth power with tangible results. The Lord led me to Isaiah 55:11. "So will my word be which goes forth from My mouth; it will not return to Me empty without accomplishing what I desire, and it will achieve the purpose for which I sent it." The Lord said to me, "My son, my word is a Messenger who is on a prospering course, and failure is not an option with Him." He said, "I can only react to my Word; the words of my people are unfruitful, which makes their prayers unfruitful in my ears, as well as unproductive in their lives."

The Lord said to me, "My son, I am called by many names, but the two which describe me truly is that I am a Pure and Spirit God. And they that worship me in prayer must use My pure words. The words of the LORD are pure words, as silver tried in the furnace of the earth, purified seven times (Psalm 12:6)."

"The words that I speak unto you they are spirit, and they are life" (John 6:63). God said to me, my son, when I look down on the earth, I view all mankind as able to be saved because of the blood of My Son Jesus. All they need to do is lay aside their pride and accept this perfect sacrifice as payment for their sins rather than try to pay the sin debt on their own. The reason I need my people to use my words in their prayer life is because my word is My Beloved Son who died for them all, and it pleases me to grant all things unto my people because of what Jesus already did once and for all. This is exactly why Jesus said in John 15:7, "If you abide in Me, and my words abide in you, ask whatever you wish, and it will be done for you." May you always put forth a quality effort to be filled with the word of God by meditating on it daily. This will greatly help you pray more effectively as a prayer warrior for Jesus Christ.

Remember this one truth, you are a prayer warrior for this generation who God will use to stand in the gap before Him to pray for agape love, churches, pastors, children, the sick, the poor, the afflicted, missions and missionaries, unbelievers, against demonic forces and spiritual wickedness in positions of government.

What is a Prayer Point?

In every scripture, there is a prayer point. The way it works is that after you read the scripture, you pray the point of prayer within that scripture. There are blessings which belongs to us as adopted children of God within each scripture. Basically, a prayer point is the blessing in every scripture being spoken upon one's life. As Jesus Christ opened the scroll in Luke 4:17-18 to the scripture concerning His life, so shall we locate our blessing in the scriptures.

CHAPTER ONE

Remaining Humble Before the Lord

The following prayers points can be used to repent of our presumptuous sins, and to take responsibility for our personal walk with the Lord. There is nothing more precious than pointing fingers at yourself before the Lord, that's humility: a place where all Christian service begins. When you humble yourself under the mighty hand of God, you will begin to experience new heights before the Lord. The Lord revealed to me that the mistakes most people make in their prayer time is jumping right into prayer without taking the time to revere and acknowledge His Holiness.

I was led by the Holy Spirit to Habakkuk 1:13, where I read the Lord's eyes are too pure to behold evil, and to look upon iniquity. Many times in the gospels, Jesus told various people suffering from sickness, disease, and other afflictions to go and sin no more. The reason is because Jesus is the True Physician. He's not going to mess around and just treat our symptoms, He deals with the root cause! Our problems are usually connected to our sins; therefore, it is always critical to take the time to confess our sins every day before entering into prayer before our Holy God.

Repenting

"He that covers his sins shall not prosper, but whosoever confesses and forsake them shall have mercy." (Proverbs 28:13)

Prayer point: "Lord, help me to not hide my sin but to have the humility to confess and forsake them each and every day before you. In Jesus' name. Amen"

"Blessed are they whose iniquities are forgiven, and whose sins are covered." (Romans 4:7a)

Prayer point: "Lord, I thank you for forgiving all my sins and covering them. In Jesus' name. Amen

"Blessed is the person whom the Lord will never count his sin against him." (Romans 4:7b)

Prayer point: "Lord, I thank you for not counting my sins against me. In Jesus' name. Amen.

"Cast me not away from your presence, and take not thy Holy Spirit away." (Psalm 51:11)

Prayer point: "Lord, do not let my sins cast me away from your presence or drive away from me your precious Holy Spirit. In Jesus' name. Amen

"Wash me thoroughly from mine iniquity, and cleanse me from my sin, O Lord. In Jesus' precious name. Amen" (Psalm 51:2)

"O Lord, have mercy upon me according to your loving kindness, and according to the multitude of your great compassion and tender mercies." (Psalm 51:1)

"Lord forgive me because I have sinned against you, and you only; have mercy on me for the evil I have done in your sight. In Jesus name. Amen."

"I, even I, am He that blots out and cancels your transgressions for my own sake, and I will not remember thy sins." (Isaiah 43:25)

Prayer point: "Lord, I pray that you will wipe away and cancel all my transgressions, and remember my sins I have committed before you. In Jesus' name. Amen."

"I have wiped out your transgressions thick as a cloud, and your sins like a heavy morning mist; return to me for I have redeemed you." (Isaiah 44:22)

Prayer point: "Lord God, I thank you for wiping out my transgressions and my sins, which are as thick as a cloud. In Jesus' name. Amen."

My personal prayer for mercy

"Lord, forgive me because I am a sinner. I have sinned against you in my thoughts and deeds. I come humbly before you as a child to ask you for mercy, so that my prayers, which are constant before You, may not be hindered. So that my relationship with you, O Lord, can never experience a drought. Lord, you are gracious and full of compassion, slow to anger and showing great mercy towards all of your children. Lord, your word says that if I confess my sins, you, O Lord are faithful and just to forgive me, and cleanse me from all my unrighteousness. Lord, I am standing before you in tears, asking for your mercy, and holding you accountable to your own words. In Jesus' name I pray. Amen."

Examine Yourself

"Examine me, O Lord, and prove me; try my reins and my heart:" (Psalm 26:2)

Most of us will never preach behind a pulpit, but I say the greatest sermon one can preach is the life they live each day. The life you and I live is like a fragrance, the question is what kind of a smell do you have on you today? Does it bring people closer to God or drive them away? Jesus said in Matthew 5:16 to "let our light shine before men, that they may see your good works, and glorify your Father which is in heaven."

These prayer points can help you become that light of the world and the salt of the earth; in Jesus' mighty name. Amen.

Paul provides us with this truly humbling scripture in his second letter to the Corinthians. When I first got saved, I hated this scripture because the truth it contained convicted my soul, and I always felt like it was written exclusively for me! I thought for sure that this verse was directed squarely at me, and it convicted my soul every time I came across it. My prayer for you is that this scripture convicts you as it did me; in Jesus' name. Amen

"Examine and test and evaluate your own selves to see whether you are holding to your faith and showing the proper fruits of it. Test and prove yourself, (not Christ) Do you not yourselves realize and know (thoroughly by an ever-increasing experience) that Jesus Christ is in you? Unless you are counterfeit, disapproved on trial and rejected." (2 Corinthians 13:5 AMP)

I tried to warn you before revealing the scripture, but the good news is that you and I are approved by the blood of Jesus Christ, and God has no plans of preventing His precious children from receiving His unfailing love.

These following prayer points will make you responsible and blameless before God and man.

"Search me, O God, and know my heart, try me, and know my thoughts in Jesus name. Amen." (Psalm 139:23-24)

Prayer point: "See if there are any wicked ways in me O Lord, and lead me in the way of everlasting joy. In Jesus' name. Amen."

"That which I see not teach thou me, if I have done iniquity, I will not do it no more." (Job 34:32)

Prayer point: "Lord, I pray that you will teach me the things which my human eyes cannot not see. I know there are things in my life that have no business there, but help me to see them, so that I can work on them. If I have done any iniquity due to what I do not see, please forgive me. In Jesus' name. Amen."

"Flee fornication. Every sin that a man does is not with the body, but he or she who commits fornication sins against his or her own body." (1 Corinthians- 6:18)

Prayer point: "Lord, I pray that you help me flee from all areas, and give me the strength and wisdom to escape every situation which tempts me to sin against my body, which is your dwelling place. In Jesus' name. Amen."

"Follow peace with all men, and holiness, without which no man shall see the Lord." (Hebrews- 12:14)

Prayer point: "Father God, help me to pursue peace with all people, and to make every effort to live a holy life. In Jesus' name. Amen."

"But the fruit of the spirit is love, joy, peace, longsuffering, gentleness, goodness, faith, meekness, temperance, against such there is no law." (Galatians- 5:22)

Prayer point: "Lord, help me to make a quality effort to acquire the fruit of your Holy Spirit. In Jesus' name. Amen."

"Therefore if God gave to them the same gift as He gave to us also after believing in the Lord Jesus Christ, who was I that I could stand in God's way?" (Acts 11:17)

Prayer point: "Lord, I pray to you this day, and request that you would remove from me any of those things I have been doing that are preventing you from using me mightily. Stop me from my own disobedience O Lord. In Jesus' name. Amen."

"So He said, 'Go forth and stand on the mountain before the Lord.' And behold, the Lord was passing by! And a great and strong wind was rending the mountains and breaking the rocks in pieces before the Lord. But the Lord was not in the wind. And after the wind an earthquake, but the Lord was not in the earthquake. After the earthquake a fire, but the Lord was not in the fire and after the fire a still small voice. Then Elijah heard it!" (1 Kings 19:11-13)

Prayer point: "Father God, help me to be sensitive towards your still small voice when you are speaking to me. I pray that you will help me to remove every loud thing which hinders my hearing your small still voice. In Jesus' name. Amen."

"Moreover it is required in stewards, that a man be found faithful." (1 Corinthians 4:1)

Prayer point: "Lord, I pray that I will be found faithful and trustworthy in all that I do in my life. In Jesus' name. Amen."

"And these things, brethren, I have in a figure transferred to myself and to Apollos for your sakes; that ye might learn in us not to think of men above that which is written, that no one of you be puffed up for one against another." (1 Corinthians 4:6)

Prayer point: "Father God, I pray away every spirit of pride arising upon my life. LORD, help me to not become puffed up. In Jesus' name. Amen."

"Walk in wisdom toward them that are without, redeeming the time." (Colossians 4:5)

Prayer point: "Lord, bless me with your divine wisdom so that I can walk in that wisdom toward all people, especially unbelievers. In Jesus' name. Amen."

"If you are willing and obedient, ye shall eat the good of the land." (Isaiah 1:19)

Prayer point: "Lord, give me a willing and obedient heart so I can eat the good of the land. In Jesus' name. Amen."

"Let your speech be always with grace, seasoned with salt, that ye may know how ye ought to answer every man." (Colossians 4:6)

Prayer point: "Lord Jesus, may you continue to bless me with words of grace when I speak to people, so that everyone who hears me will be blessed due to my gracious answer. In Jesus' name. Amen."

"For thou wilt light my candle: the Lord my God will enlighten my darkness." (Psalm 18:28)

Prayer point: "Lord, enlighten my darkness and turn it into your marvelous light. In Jesus' precious name. Amen."

CHAPTER 2
Praying for Strength and Patience

Apostle Paul compares the Christian life to running a race in 1 Corinthians 9:24, where he asks this question, "Do you not know that those who run in a race all run, but one receives the prize? Run in such a way that you may win."

As we examine this passage I want to point out that not all races are the same. Some races are relay races, while in others the runner starts and finishes. Some races have hurdles. The races are also different distances ranging from a 100-yard dash to a marathon. In some races, the runner has a lane he stays in while others do not have a specific lane.

I would like to encourage you to stay in your own lane when running your race. Since we are all different, God may have a different race for you to run then he does for me. This is often based on a Christian's experience level. It would be unfair to take a new runner and put him in a marathon. My experiences are different than yours and yours are different than mine. We hinder ourselves when we start to compare our personal races, lifestyles, standards, social status, and reputation to that of others. Stay in your own lane and run the course that God has set for you. The book of Hebrews makes this clear in this striking verse!

"Let us lay aside every weight, and the sin which doth so easily beset us, and let us run with patience the race that is set before us." (Hebrews 12:1)

Notice the verse differentiates between weights and the sin that easily entangles us. Sin is something that is a violation of God's law and standards for us, and it is universal; meaning what is a sin for one is a sin for all. However, a weight is something that is not necessarily a sin but will keep you from performing your best. For example, suppose I showed up on the race track and while everyone was getting ready, I put on a pair of shoulder pads and a helmet. While there is nothing wrong with me doing this, I will not be able to run as fast as I could if I didn't have these things on. Likewise, there are things in your life that are not sins but they will slow you down and prevent you from performing your best, and could prevent you from winning the race God has set before you.

For some people, it could be the news. There is nothing wrong with reading a newspaper or watching the news on television, but if it starts to take up too much of your time and prevent you from spending time in the word of God and prayer, then it has become a weight for you. Someone else can watch and read the news and be able to maintain a balance over it. For them, news is not a weight but it is for the other person. The same is true of too many things to mention, be it sports, leisure time, fellowshipping, even spending too much time serving God. That last one might shock you, but it is true. There are many ministers across this country who spend so much time serving the ministry of God that they have neglected the God of the ministry. Anything that prevents you from running your race effectively is a weight, whether that weight is good or bad.

Solomon teaches us that "the race is not to the swift, nor the battle to the strong, nor bread to the wise, nor riches to men of understanding, nor favor to men of skill (Ecclesiastes 9:11). But it is all due to the time which God permits us while running this race, and the blessed chances which our heavenly Father grants to all His children who are on this journey.

When Jesus sent out His disciples in Matthew 10:21, He warned them they would be hated by all men for His sake. He said, "but it is he or she who endures to the end that shall be saved." We need to endure, my brothers and sisters. The bible says bodily exercise profits little, but godliness is profitable in all things (1 Timothy 4:8). We need to build up some spiritual muscles so we can run and finish this race (1 Kings 19:5-7). Even the great Elijah needed some angelic assistance as he laid down in fatigue and distress and fear. Twice, the angel of the Lord had to wake him up to eat and drink while on his journey. The angel said to Elijah "arise and eat for the journey is too great." After eating the meal the angel prepared, it sustained Elijah for forty days and forty nights.

May you also go in the strength of your heavenly provision in Jesus' name. The journey to follow Christ is very challenging and filled with many dangers and trials, but we can rejoice and be exceedingly glad when God gives us the divine strength and patience to endure to the end, where we will receive our crown of righteousness from Our Master, Lord Jesus Christ; who is the Author and Finisher of our journey in Him. Praise the Lord people!

I want to encourage you to make it a daily habit to pray for the two virtues that will guarantee you a sure ending and a good victory on this great journey.

The following prayer points will prompt the Lord to strengthen you daily with the patience needed to endure until the end.

"If thou faint or falter in the day of adversity, thy strength is small! you need strength, ask god for it." (Proverbs 24:10)

"But Jesus answered Satan, and said, it is written, Man shall not live by bread alone, but by every word that proceeds out of the mouth of God." (Matthew 4:4)

Prayer point: "Lord Jesus, help me to meditate and delight myself in your word daily. Help me to put forth more effort to read my bible. In Jesus' name. Amen."

"But you shall receive power, ability, efficiency, might, and strength after the Holy Ghost has come upon you." (Acts 1:8)

Prayer point: "Lord, I invite your precious Holy Spirit into my life. Holy Spirit, I acknowledge your presence in my life, and I need you to strengthen me with power. In Jesus' name. Amen."

"God is my strength and power, he makes my way perfect." (2 Samuel- 22.33)

Prayer point: "Lord be my strength and my power in everything. Make my way perfect. In Jesus' name. Amen."

"In the day when I cried, you answered me, and strengthened me with strength in my soul." (Psalm 138:3)

Prayer point: "Lord, strengthen my soul; keep my soul fit for this race that is before me. In Jesus' name. Amen."

Most of the times that Satan attempts to discourage our efforts concerning the Lord's work, is the perfect time for us prayer warriors to come out swinging at the devil using prayer points.

"For they made us afraid, saying, their hands shall be weakened from the work, that it be not done. Now therefore, O God, strengthen my hands." (Nehemiah 6:9)

Prayer point: "Father God, strengthen my hands to continue to do your work so I can fight and pray, and to give more when my finances are being attacked, and to love more, even though people have hurt me. In Jesus' name. Amen."

"So God dealt well with the midwives and the people multiply, and became very strong." (Exodus 1:20)

Prayer point: "Lord, I know that you are the God of multiplication, and I know that you will multiply my abilities and make me strong on this journey. In Jesus' name. Amen."

"But I discipline my body and make it my slave, so that after I have preached to others, I myself will not be disqualified." (1 Corinthians 9:27)

Prayer point: "Lord, give me the strength to discipline my body and make it a slave unto me, so that I will not be disqualified from the prize. In Jesus' name. Amen.

"Keep thy tongue from evil, and thy lips from speaking guile or deceit." (Psalm 34:13-14)

Prayer point: "Lord, give me the strength to keep my tongue and lips from speaking evil things and lies. In Jesus' name. Amen."

"Depart from evil, and do good, seek peace, and pursue it." (Psalm 34:14)

Prayer point: "Lord, give me the strength to depart from all evil, and to do good, seek peace, and pursue only your righteousness. In Jesus' name. Amen.

Prayer point: "Lord, I pray that you would bless me with the spirit of patience to wait on your promises through your Son Jesus Christ. In Jesus' name. Amen."

Prayer point: "Lord, help me to not make hasty decisions concerning my life. In Jesus' name. Amen."

"Trust in the Lord with all thine heart, and lean not on your own understanding. In all thy ways acknowledge Him, and he shall direct thy paths." (Proverbs 3:5)

Prayer points: "Father God, help me to have the patience to consult you in prayer concerning my path in life, so that I do not lean on my own understanding. In Jesus' name. Amen."

"The righteous shall not be afraid of bad news; his heart is steadfast, trusting in the Lord. His heart is secure, he will have no fear." (Psalm 112:7-8)

Prayer point: "Lord, help me to never be shaken by bad news. I pray that you will help me to trust in you more during my times of trouble. Lord, I pray for a secure heart in your promise, and to be a fearless servant for you O Lord. In Jesus' name. Amen."

"Bear one another's burdens, and thereby fulfill the law of Christ." (Galatians- 6:2)

Prayer point: "Father God, give me the patience to be a burden bearer like Christ, and to be a great help to others in need. Lord, help me to live a selfless life like Jesus Christ. In Jesus' name. Amen."

"Let us not be weary in well doing; for in due season we shall reap, if we faint not." (Galatians 6:9)

Prayer point: "Lord, bless me with the patience to continue doing well in life. In Jesus' name. Amen."

"But none of these things move me, neither count my life dear unto myself, so that I might finish my course with joy, and the ministry, which I have received of the Lord Jesus, to testify the gospel of the grace of God." (Acts 20:24)

Prayer point: "Lord, bless me with the patience to finish my race, and the ministry which you have given me on earth, with joy. In Jesus' name. Amen."

Prayer point: "Lord, give me the patience to finish my education, to teach my children your word, and to keep my job even though my heart is not there. In Jesus' name. Amen."

"As you know how we exhorted and comforted and charged every one of you, as a father does to his children. That you would walk worthy of God, who hath called you unto his kingdom and glory." (1 Thessalonians 2:11-12)

Prayer point: "Lord, give me the patience to continue walking worthy of you each day of my life. In Jesus' name. Amen."

"And that we may be delivered from unreasonable and wicked men. For all men have not the faith." (2 Thessalonians 3:2)

Prayer point: "Father God, give me the patience to love wicked and unreasonable managers and co-workers, peers or so-called friends, families, ex-boyfriends, and ex-girlfriends, church members, law officials, government officials, pastors, and all other people. In Jesus' name. Amen."

CHAPTER 3
Praying for Divine Favor

"The blessings of the Lord makes one rich, and He adds no sorrow to it," the bible tells us in Proverbs 10:22. Let me take this time to speak to your spirit man, as the Holy Spirit is leading me to say. If you or anyone is experiencing sorrow along with their blessings, then that blessing is not from the Lord of peace. I am happy to say that we serve a God who truly blesses His children, and his blessings come with no sorrow or burden, but only an overflowing of heavenly joy in one's heart at the reception of it. When we experience God's divine blessings, favor, prosperity, or goodness, it will be clear that it was the Lord's doing. No relatives, spouses, friends, employer, social status, or money will be able to take the glory. God says that He will not share his glory with anyone (Isaiah 42:8).

Divine favor is the unspoken and hidden dream of every human being. It is God enabling the upward movement or forwardness of His children. If there is anything we all need at this time, it is God's divine blessings, favor, prosperity, and His goodness. Let's be honest, you and I can never work hard enough to acquire everything we deserve, neither can we work long enough to be totally debt free. Even if you pay for your house, you still have property taxes you have to pay every year. I want to remind you that what God is about to accomplish in your life is an act of His goodness towards you based the kind of prayer He receives from you.

The prayer points in this chapter will encourage God to jump ahead of the waiting line for your sake. Praise the Lord! One day of experiencing God's provision is worth a lifetime of labor. King David confirms to us in Psalm 37:25, "I have been young, and now I am old; yet I have never seen the righteous forsaken, nor his seed begging for bread." In Jesus name, you my righteous good friend will not be the first to beg for bread. Amen. My prayer is that you will experience God's hand upon your life in all aspects of your life. In Jesus' name. Amen. "Beloved, I pray that you may prosper in every way and that your body may keep well, even as i know your soul keeps well and prosper." (3 John 1:2)

May you always pray using these following prayer points, which were chosen by the Holy Ghost to remind God of the promises made to father Abraham in Genesis 12:2-3. "And I will make of thee a great nation, and bless thee, and make thy name great, and thou shalt be a blessing. and

I will bless them that bless thee, and curse them that curseth thee, and in thee shall all families of the earth be blessed."

May these prayer points help you to always experience the Lord's divine blessedness, favor, prosperity, and goodness in your life daily. In Jesus' name. Amen.

"And Abraham was old and stricken in age; and the Lord had blessed Abraham in all things." (Genesis 24:1)

Prayer point: "Lord, I pray that you would bless me in all things like you did with father Abraham. Not just in certain areas O Lord, but in all things. In Jesus' mighty name. Amen."

"And the Lord was with Joseph, and he was a prosperous man; and he was in the house of his master the Egyptian." (Genesis 39:2)

Prayer point: "Lord, be with me. Make me become prosperous like your servant Joseph. In Jesus' name. Amen."

"And his master saw that the Lord was with him, and that the Lord made all that he did to prosper in his hands." (Genesis 39:2)

Prayer point: "Father God, may people see and take notice of your presence in my life. I pray that you will make all that I do to prosper in my hands. In Jesus' name. Amen."

"But the Lord was with Joseph, and showed him mercy, and gave him favor in the sight of the keeper of the prison." (Genesis 39:21)

Prayer point: "Lord, be with my life, show me your loving kindness, mercy, and favor in the sight of my enemies. In Jesus' name. Amen."

"Thus said the Lord, thy Redeemer, the Holy One of Israel; I am the LORD thy God which teaches thee to profit, which leads thee by the way that thou should go." (Isaiah 48:17)

Prayer point: "Lord, teach me how to profit in life, and lead me to my divine destiny. In Jesus' name. Amen."

"Now it came about in the thirtieth year, on the fifth day of the fourth month, while I was by the river of Cherbar among the exiles, the heavens were opened and I saw visions of God." (Ezekiel 1:1)

Prayer point: "Lord, I pray for open heavens upon my life. Let everything that concerns me operate under open heavens. My children, job, driving, church, friends, loved ones, my future, my thoughts, my heart, marriage; may all function under open heavens. In Jesus' name. Amen."

"For it is you who blesses the righteous man, O lord, You surround him with favor as with a shield." (Psalm 5:12)

Prayer point: "Lord, surround me with divine favor. May your divine favor become my daily protection. In Jesus' name. Amen."

"Thou shalt increase my greatness, and comfort me on every side." (Psalm 71:21)

Prayer point: "Lord increase my greatness when I am troubled on every side, so you may comfort me on every side. In Jesus' name. Amen."

"Think upon me, my God, for good, and according to all that I have done for this people." (Nehemiah 5:19)

Many times, we are led by the Holy Spirit to do gracious acts in people's lives, but never receive a thank you for our efforts. Let me remind you that all the good we do is only because we love God, and therefore have the mind of Christ. God will thank you abundantly when people cannot be trusted to show their appreciation.

Prayer point: "Lord, I pray that you would think upon me for all the good I have done and continue to do for others, and remember me in my time of need. In Jesus' name. Amen."

"He has swallowed down riches, and he shall vomit them up again: God shall cast them out of his belly." (Job 20:15)

Prayer point: "Lord, I pray that you would make the devil vomit out all my stolen riches. May all of my stolen blessings be cast out of his slippery belly. In Jesus' name. Amen."

"He blesses them and they multiply greatly, and He does not let their cattle decrease." (Psalm 107:38)

Prayer point: "Father God, bless my life. Make me to multiply greatly, and I pray against decrease coming against my increase. In Jesus' name. Amen."

"Show me a sign of your evident goodwill and favor that those who hate me may see it and be put to shame, because You, Lord will your approval of me when you help and comfort me." (Psalm 86:17)

Prayer point: "Lord, show me a sign of your goodness so that my enemies will see it and be put to shame. In Jesus' name. Amen.

"And to the angel of the church in Philadelphia write: These things said he that is holy, he that is true, he that has the key of David, he that opens, and no man shuts, and shuts, and no man opens." (Revelation 3:7)

The Lord is revealing to me that there are doors which are going to be opened in your life as well as some doors you need to shut.

Open These Doors

Prayer point: "Lord, I pray that you will open doors of peace, blessings, joy, riches, favor, your goodness, divine health, wisdom, knowledge, fresh anointing, and obedient children. In Jesus' name. Amen."

Close These Doors

Prayer point: "Lord, I pray that you will close doors of fear, complacency, poverty, sickness, joblessness, bad luck, failure, setbacks, corruption, sexual perversion, pride, anger, deceit, fornication, marital problems, unfruitfulness, drunkenness, drug addictions, smoking, cursing, and all worldly lust and desires. In Jesus' name. Amen."

"For your shame you shall have double; and for confusion they shall rejoice in their portion: therefore in their land they shall possess the double everlasting joy shall be unto them." (Isaiah 61:7)

Prayer point: "Lord, I pray and decree, and declare this day, that each time Satan causes me shame, that shame shall turn into a double blessing for me. In Jesus' name. Amen."

"For He performs the thing that is appointed for me, and many such things are with him." (Job 23:14)

Prayer point: "Father God, I pray that You, O God, shall manifest all the things which are appointed for me, and for my life. Let my appointed blessings be performed immediately. In Jesus' name. Amen."

"For I will set my eyes upon them for good, and I will bring them again to this land; and I will build them up, and not pull them down, and I will plant them, and not pluck them up." (Jeremiah 24:6)

Prayer point: "Lord, I pray that you will set your precious eyes upon my life, my children, my marriage, job, church, families, when I am driving, my finances, this nation, and all that concerns me for God. In Jesus' name. Amen.

"And David went and grew great, and the Lord God of host was with him." (2 Samuel 5:10)

Prayer point: "Father God, make me to grow in grace. Help me to excel in growing my children, my businesses, my loved ones, and my career. Give me more of your wisdom, knowledge, and increase my ministry and strengthen my marriage. In Jesus' name. Amen."

"For I will pour water upon him that is thirsty, and floods upon the dry ground: I will pour my spirit upon thy seed, and my blessings upon thing offspring." (Isaiah 44:3)

Prayer point: "Lord, I pray your heavenly flood upon every dry area of my life. Flood my dry ground O Lord. In Jesus' name. Amen."

"But you shall be named the Priest of the Lord; you will be spoken of as minister of our God. You will eat the riches of the gentiles, and in their riches you will boast." (Isaiah 61:6)

Prayer point: "Lord, your word said that I will eat the riches of the gentiles, and the wealth of nations. Your word also says that I will boast in their riches. I am holding you accountable O Lord, for your words concerning my life. In Jesus' name. Amen."

"May the Lord, the God of your fathers, increase you a thousand times and bless you as He has promised." (Deuteronomy 1:8)

Prayer point: "Lord, God make me a thousand times greater as you have promised. In Jesus' name. Amen."

CHAPTER 4

Praying for Our Children

Our topic in this chapter is one which makes me emotional with love, but aggressive in how I respond when our blessed children are threatened. I am emotional about this topic because I am the proud father of four wonderful children God gave me. Kayla, my oldest daughter, reminded me when she was three years old that smoking was bad for me. Nehemiah, who believes his daddy when he told him that he was born to build houses for God. Naomi, who is my self-proclaimed princess based on the outfit she wore for her fourth birthday party. Then last, but not least, is my youngest boy, who I called Prophet Nathan, aka the prophet of our time, by God's grace. Trust me when I say, that I truly feel God has blessed me with such precious children to call my own. Those, who like me, have been blessed to have children can relate to my excitement. If you do not have children, I will pray in advance for you to be blessed with them and also, for their well-being once they have entered the world. In Jesus' name.

I also said that this topic makes me aggressive. I am not referring to how I treat my children, but in how I respond daily in prayer concerning them. You would be wise to do the same thing. Satan comes to steal, kill, and to destroy our children's minds by attempting to prevent them from knowing God, which leads them to disobey their parents and others in authority. I don't know about you, but if I was the devil, angry over losing my position in God's kingdom and unable to go back to heaven, I would do everything I could to prevent everyone else from getting in. The way I would accomplish this would be to hit God's people where it hurts them the most, their children.

We see this played out in Job chapter 1. When Satan went after all of Job's possessions, he started with the animals but the last thing he did was kill his children. The reason is, Satan was saving the best for last. Children are Satan's secret weapon then, and most especially now. Job experienced many losses, but when his children were killed, he lashed out in an aggressive manner, but he still did not become bitter at God. We can only hope and pray for the courage of job during our times of horror.

Children are a gift from the Lord. They are the fruit of the womb according to the word of God in Deuteronomy 28:4. They are a reward from God, and they are a tradition towards His blessed people as promised in His word. We are living in a time when the devil knows his time is short. It has been said that desperate times call for desperate measures, and the devil's wrath is more intense in these last days. His diabolical plan today is a scorched earth policy against our children. There is a reason why little Billy, Susan, and Tyrone are not doing so well at home and school like they used to. One of the many signs of the end times are people, including children, displaying an exceptional level of disobedience to those in positions of authority and being unthankful. This pretty much describes children in the world today.

Parents, allow me to speak boldly to your hearts. If we do not invest time praying for our children, the devil, who is the god of this world, will invest his time in providing them with role models who are not godly, and he will fill their minds with worldly thoughts and turn them away from God.

Paul writes to us in Ephesians 2:2, "wherein in time past you walked according to the course of this world, according to the prince of the power of the air, the spirit that now worked in the children of disobedience." Disobedience is a spirit, and like other evil spirits, the devil is diligently sprinkling this foul spirit throughout our air, and it is very contagious and destructive once it enters a child. How many times do we celebrate a young man or woman heading to college, only to mourn at their funeral six months later due to some foul act they committed during their transition period? Perhaps many of these tragedies could have been avoided if, in Jesus' name, we would have prayed down the fury of God upon the spirit of disobedience that is leading our children astray. I urge all of us who are mature Christians to engage in daily times of prayer over our children.

The following prayer points are chosen by the Spirit of the living God for us to use in our prayer sessions concerning the well-being and protection of our children from all the works of Satan.

"To Jesus the mediator of a new covenant, and to the sprinkled of blood that speaks better things or word than the blood of Abel." (Hebrews 12:24)

Prayer point: "Father God, may the blood of your Son Jesus speak better things in the life of my children. Let the blood of Jesus Christ speak a better word concerning my children. In Jesus' name. Amen."

"The blood will be sign for you on the houses where you are; and **when I (God) see the blood, I will pass over you**. No destructive plague will touch you when I strike Egypt." (Exodus 12:13)

Prayer point: "Lord, I cover all my children with the mighty blood of Jesus Christ: Father God, your word says that when You see the blood upon my children, addictions, disobedience, anger, fear, suicidal tendencies, generational curses, sicknesses, and diseases, discouragement, failure, cancer, high blood pressure, and heart attack shall pass over them. In Jesus' name. amen."

"Keep, watch over, or guard your heart with all diligence, for out of it are the issues of life." (Proverbs 4:23)

Prayer point: "Lord, give my children the wisdom to watch over their hearts in all that they do in life. In Jesus' name. Amen."

"It would be better for him to be thrown into the sea with a milestone tied around his neck than for him to cause one of these little ones to sin or stumble." (Luke 17:2)

Prayer point: "I pray O Lord, that whosoever causes my children to stumble away from your teaching, and leads them to sin against you, shall greatly sink in deep waters along with their burdens. In Jesus' name. Amen."

"So give your servant an understanding heart to judge Your people to discern between good and evil. For who is able to judge this great people of yours." (1 Kings 3:9)

Prayer point: "Lord, if you can do anything for me, I pray that all my children will have an understanding heart, and the ability to know the difference between good and evil while they are faced with so many people every day. In Jesus' name. Amen."

"It was for freedom that Christ set us free; therefore keep standing firm and do not be subject again to a yoke of slavery." (Galatians 5:1)

Prayer point: "Lord God, I pray against every evil thing that is contrary to your purpose of freedom concerning my children. I pray that whatever threatens or hinders the freedom you have given my children will be dissolved by your Holy Ghost fire. In Jesus' name. Amen.

"O foolish Galatians, who has bewitched, or cast a spell on you, that you should not obey the truth, before whose eyes Jesus Christ has been evidently set for, crucified among you?" (Galatians 3:1)

Prayer point: "Father God, I loose every witchcraft activity directed at my children in the name of Jesus, and I destroy every demonic spell cast upon my children, in the mighty name of Jesus Christ. Amen.

"Be gracious to me, O Lord; See my affliction from those who hate me, You who lift me from the gates of death." (Psalm 9:13)

Prayer point: "Lord, be gracious to my children; see their afflictions by all those who hate them, and lift my children from the gates of death, so that premature death shall not be their portion. In Jesus' name. Amen."

"That the God of our Lord Jesus Christ, the Father of glory, may give unto you the spirit of wisdom and revelation in the knowledge of Him. That the eyes of your understanding being enlightened; that you may know what the hope of his calling is, and what the riches of His inheritance in the saints." (Ephesians 1:17-18)

Prayer point: "Lord God, I pray for wisdom and revelation of Your knowledge upon my children, and that their spiritual eyes may be enlightened to your divine will and purpose for them. In Jesus' name. Amen."

"I shall not die, but shall live, and declare the works of the Lord." (Psalm 118:17)

Prayer point: "I pray in the mighty name of Jesus that my children shall not die, but live to proclaim the good news, and be used mightily by God. In Jesus' name. Amen."

"Thou hast enlarged my steps under me that my feet did not slip." (Psalm 18:36)

Prayer point: "Father God, enlarge the steps of my children, so that their feet cannot slip. In Jesus' name. Amen."

"He delivered me from mine enemies: yea, thou liftest me above those that rise up against me; thou hast delivered me from the violent man." (Psalm 18:48)

Prayer point: "Lord, lift my children above all their enemies and deliver them from every violent person or act. In Jesus' mighty name. Amen."

"By humility and the fear of the Lord are riches, and honor, and life." (Proverbs 22:4)

Prayer point: "Lord I pray to you that You, O Lord, will give my children a humble heart to fear You always. In Jesus' name. Amen"

"I will go before thee, and make the crooked places straight: I will break in pieces the gates of brass, and cut in sunder the bars of iron." (Isaiah 45:2)

Prayer point: "Lord, I command that you go before my children and make every crooked place straight in their lives. In Jesus' name. Amen."

"Keep me as the apple of the eye, hide me under the shadow of thy wings." (Psalm 17:8)

Prayer point: "Lord God, keep my children as the apple of your eyes, and hide them always under the shadow of your wings. In Jesus name. Amen."

"Our fathers have sinned, and are not and we have borne their iniquities." (Lamentation 5:7)

Prayer point: "Lord, I ask you to remove and destroy every generational sin or curse attached to my children. In Jesus name. Amen."

"As for me, I will behold thy face in righteousness: I shall be satisfied, when I awake, with thy likeness." (Psalm 17:15)

Prayer point: "Lord Jesus, I pray that my children will awake to your likeness each blessed day. In Jesus' name. Amen."

"Epaphras, who is one of you, a servant of Christ salute you always, laboring fervently for you in prayers, that you may stand perfect and complete in all the will of God." (Colossians 4:12)

Prayer point: "Lord, I am praying fervently unto You O LORD for my children to stand perfect and complete in Your perfect will. In Jesus' name. Amen."

"Enter not into the path of the wicked, and go not in the way of evil men." (Proverbs 4:14)

Prayer point: "Lord, grant unto my children Your wisdom to avoid every path and every way of the evil one. In Jesus' name. Amen."

"I have stuck unto thy testimonies lord put me not to shame." (Psalm 119:31)

Prayer point: "Lord, I am thy faithful servant. May my children be excluded from the shame of Satan. In Jesus' name. Amen."

"And now, brethren, I command you to God, and to the word of his grace, which is able to build you up, and to give you an inheritance among all them which are sanctified." (Acts 20:35)

Prayer point: "I commend all my unsaved children, and those of my loved ones, to God in the name of Jesus. Amen."

"And that we may be delivered from unreasonable and wicked men, for all men have not the faith." (2 Thessalonians 3:2)

Prayer point: "Father God, may all my children be delivered from unreasonable and wicked people in every area life takes them. In Jesus' name. Amen."

"Turn, O backsliding children, said the Lord; for I am married unto you; and I will take you of a city, and two of a family, and I will you pastors according to mine heart which will feed you with knowledge and understanding." (Jeremiah 3:14)

Prayer point: "Lord, I pray the blood of Jesus upon the spirit of backsliding that has tormented my children. May my children return back to Your house and submit their lives to You. Lord, bring mentors into their life and pastors after Your own heart to lead them on the path of righteousness. In Jesus' name. Amen."

CHAPTER 5

Praying Against the Spirit of Being Hindered

I remember the first time I was given the chance to pray at a retreat in Buffalo, New York. I was so excited, but I never knew why I felt this way, being so new to the things of ministry. When I opened my mouth to pray, I could not help but direct all my prayers towards the devil and rebuking him upon the lives of those attending the retreat. After the service was over, several ministers and strangers approached me with gladness in their hearts, letting me know they appreciated my having a warrior spirit, and that my prayer was exactly what they needed. I replied in a humble manner to all of them, but in my heart I knew that the spirit world had taken note of a fairly new, ordained soldier for Christ for this generation.

I believe God has given me a warrior spirit to fight Satan, and the only way to be successful in this battle is to pray fervently using the word of God. The devil and I know each other very well, but my fear is that many Christians know about Satan but they do not know him. Jesus teaches us in Matthew 10:28, "Do not fear those who kill the body but are not able to kill the soul, but rather fear Him who is able to destroy both soul and body in hell." My brothers and sisters in Christ, our enemy is not physical, but spiritual, therefore we do not use physical weapons to defeat him, but spiritual weapons.

No wise military leader engages the enemy without first conducting a proper reconnaissance. When General Patton won a victory over Field Marshal Erwin Rommel, one of Germany's greatest generals, he said one of the keys to victory was that "I read your book;" a reference to "*The Tank in Attack*," which is still required reading at military schools today. To properly fight your enemy, you must take the time to know your enemy, and by doing so you will find out three things.

1. Knowledge of your true enemy; Satan, the devil, serpent, dragon, false prophet, and many other names. Your enemy is not other people or the government, they are simply pawns being used by the real enemy.
2. Knowledge of the enemy's weapons; deception, lies, destruction, killing, evil, wickedness, theft, and hindrances.
3. Knowledge of how the enemy uses his weapons; diligently and effectively.

During my five years of active ministry, I blessed God and am persuaded of my calling, which is a prayer warrior who just happens to be blessed with the gift to preach, according to the Lord's voice to me while I was standing in the library waiting for a computer to type this book!

Our focus in this chapter is on Satan's ability to hinder.

Hindering is defined as "to be or get in the way of, to obstruct or delay the progress of, and to interfere with an action."

While this definition is accurate, for us to better understand this word regarding our spiritual battles, and why the devil uses this tactic, we must refer to the Greek definition of the word.

In Greek, the word Hinder is Egkopto, but there are two meanings to it.

1. It refers to a road so badly broken up that it is impassible
2. It also draws the picture of a runner cutting in or elbowing a fellow runner out of the way.

Now we can see why Satan uses hindering as part of his arsenal. He does not want God's people to endure to the end in their individual races, so he works diligently to block our narrow way and knock us off the path of righteousness!

Apostle Paul, who knows all too well about this topic, revealed to the church of Thessalonica how Satan attempted to stop him. "For we wanted to come to you more than once, and yet Satan Hindered us." (1 Thessalonians 2:18)

The devil is after everyone who is attempting or moving upward in Christ Jesus. My sincere prayer is that God will create a detour for every road block you will face, in Jesus' name. My prayers for you are also that for every attempt the devil makes to try and get you off your path of destiny, that God Almighty will block all his efforts. In Jesus' name. Amen.

My humble prayer for you as you enjoy the blessings of the prayer points in this chapter is for the Living God to always provide a way back on the path for every roadblock you face. In Jesus' name. Amen.

The bible says when Paul and Silas prayed and sang praises unto God, immediately all the prison doors were opened and every chain became unfastened, or loosed (Acts 16:26). Hallelujah! Praise the Lord.

Prayer point: "Father, in the name of Jesus Christ, I pray and decree in the spirit for all locked doors currently in my life to be immediately opened in the name of Jesus. I also pray for every demonic chain holding and choking my destiny to be immediately loosed and unfastened in the mighty name of Jesus Christ. Amen."

The bible says Isaac experienced some difficulties, or setbacks and hindrances in his attempt to dig a well: "So Isaac attempted for a third time, and was successful, so he named the well REHOBOTH, which means ROOM" (Genesis 26:22). Isaac said, for now the Lord has made room for us, and we shall be fruitful in the land. Praise the Lord somebody.

Prayer point: "Lord God, I pray that every failed opportunity due to Satan's hindering me shall finally come to pass in Jesus' name. Lord, I pray that You O Lord will make room in my many failed attempts. Lord I know you will make room for me to get hired at the company of my desire, and that you will make room for my gifts to be recognized by great people. Lord, I pray that even though there are many are ahead of me in this process, You my God will make me the head and not the tail. In Jesus' name. Amen."

"Now Jericho a fenced town with high walls because of the children of Israel, it was tightly closed. No one went out or came in" (Joshua 6:1). From this chapter, we know that this was the first real test for God's people. The city of Jericho was well-known and respected in the ancient world. It had a great wall that was considered impenetrable. This wall was a hindrance in their progression to conquer the Promised Land that God had given them. As New Testament believers, we can be certain that our Lord Jesus does not hinder us from progressing. He says to us in John 10:9, "I am the door, and by me if any man enter in he shall be saved, and shall go in and out, and find pasture." Blessed be the Lord for the freedom we have in Him, but sadly, many believers and unbelievers are not moving as freely as they ought to according to the promise of God because of their own personal Jericho wall.

God was not concerned with the threat posed by the people inside the wall, His focus was on bringing the wall down. Hallelujah! Let me remind you that in the Old Testament we could physically see the enemies of God, but in the New Testament, our walls of Jericho are invisible but with visible effects. The walls of Jericho represent every high thing which exalts itself against the knowledge of God in our lives, it must be brought down to the obedience of Christ.

Your Jericho walls may be your addiction to smoking, drinking, sex, pornography, cursing, anger, lying, adultery, fame, money etc.

Whatever has dominated your life for so long and is hindering your progression to reaching your full potential in Christ is your wall of Jericho. These great walls may look physically impassible, but in the spirit they are tumbling down in Jesus' name. The bible asks, "is there anything too hard for God?" I encourage you to take the shield of faith, which will enable you to extinguish all the flaming arrows of the evil one in all your efforts to bring the wall down (Ephesians 6:16).

This is your time and season to truly walk in the Liberty of Jesus Christ that God has given us, along with the power to crush and demolish every high Jericho wall in the mighty name of Jesus. Tell the devil your case is different. And that all his apples have worms, and in the name of Jesus Christ, you don't want them any longer.

The Lord is telling me to remind you that temptations are just suggestions and you can either say yes or no to them. When Satan places them in your path, say "get behind me Satan for the Lord rebukes you in the name of Jesus."

Keep this verse in your mind: "You can do all things through Christ which strengthens you." (Philippians 4:13)

Blessed be God, for I see your walls of Jericho coming down instantly in the mighty name of Jesus Christ. I speak the blood of Jesus Christ against it.

Now start thanking the Lord for your victory: "Lord, I thank you because I can see my Jericho wall tumbling like dust under my feet in Jesus' name. Thank You Lord, because I can see my destiny, a better marriage, happy children, healthier living, a free mind rid of the trash of Satan."

Remember this beloved brothers and sisters, during your prayer sessions, Satan will be diligently fighting back because he desires to have your soul and wants to prevent you from serving God and getting eternal rewards. But no matter what my brothers and sisters, pray diligently and fight for your freedom, which is the reason Christ died for you. I am with you in the spirit, and as I am writing this, I feel your heart as you are reading this chapter, and it is more determined than ever. The truth is, all we have belongs to God; we were created to be free so we can worship Him in the beauty of His holiness.

"For I consider that the suffering of this present time are not worthy to be compared with the glory which shall be revealed in us." (Romans 8:18)

"Now Naaman, Captain of the host of the king of Syria was a great man with his master, and honorable, because by him the Lord had given deliverance unto Syria: he was also a mighty man in valor, BUT he had leprosy." (2 Kings 5:1)

My focus in this text is not on the many accomplishments of Captain Naaman, instead I wish to expose the three-letter word which overlooks all his accomplishments, skills, and abilities. Many people, believers and unbelievers, suffer from this three-letter word in their daily lives.

BUT is a negative conjunction which is defined as being contrary: It is usually used right after a positive or inspirational statement. I will use myself as an example to further express my aim. In high school, I was a big football player; strong, fast, and naturally gifted, but I could not focus on practices or put forth the effort I needed to be successful. My excuse when people asked me would be, "Yes I was great and could have made it to the NFL, BUT my father and mother never made it to my practices and games." We use this word to make excuses for our own personal letdowns and failures. I was very good at using it for a long time. One thing I have learned from being a soldier of Christ is that "excuses are the curses of the uncommitted."

Captain Naaman was great at many things, and he was a wonderful and mighty man, BUT he had leprosy, which was his one blemish. I am telling you today that the blood of Jesus Christ has erased every blemish from our lives once and for all. I Imagine Jesus hanging on the cross after saying "It is finished" then immediately adding, "but not until we add a little to it!" God forbid this curse and contrary word of Satan from our lives in Jesus' mighty name.

We are certain that the Lord Jesus Christ finished salvation's plan by paying our sin debt by becoming sin for us (2 Corinthians 5:21). There is no mention in scripture of their being something else necessary for salvation and for us to obtain victory in Christ. My bible says in Philippians 4:13 that we can do all things through Christ which strengthens us. There is nothing contrary to the truth of God's word. The word BUT should not be a part of believer's vocabulary. Jesus came so that we might have life and have it more abundantly. How does one learn the protocols of a kingdom if they have not first experienced it? I pray that this word BUT will not hinder you from living this abundant life in Christ. There is no BUT attached to the promises of God. The bible tells us in 2 Chronicles 26:5 concerning King Uzziah who assumed the throne at the age of 16 that as long as he sought The Lord God, God made him prosperous. When we diligently seek the Lord first in all things, God is busy working diligently for us.

"For the eyes of the lord run to and fro throughout the whole earth showing himself strong on behalf of those who heart is perfect, or blameless, or completely, or fully committed to him." (2 Chronicles 16:9)

Anything that is contrary to the word of God is from Satan, and I command it all to be extinguished by the fury fire of the Lord. In Jesus' name. Amen. There is no BUT attached to your destiny. The Lord's plans concerning your life shall come to pass in Jesus' name. Every BUT that has held you back or hindered your progression is consumed by fire and erased in Jesus name. Every contrary or lying spirit standing against your divine opportunities is uprooted by the finger of the Living God. In Jesus' name. Amen.

"This is what the Lord says to His anointed (Cyrus), whose right hand I take hold of to subdue nations before him and to strip kings of their armor, and to open doors before him so that gates will not be shut." (Isaiah 45:1)

In this prayer point, I need you to substitute Cyrus' name for yours and pray, "O Lord, go before me and open all doors which Satan has shut in my life. In the name of Jesus Christ, no gates shall be shut in my pursuit of divine purpose. Amen."

"Therefore thy gates shall not be open continually; they shall not be shut day or night; that men may bring unto thee the forces of the Gentiles; and that their kings may be brought." (Isaiah 61:11)

Prayer point: "Lord, I pray that my gates of divine favor and blessings from my open heavens shall continue to be opened day and night. In Jesus' name. Amen."

I feel your spirit as you read this chapter, and Satan is trembling right now in Jesus' name.

God is troubling me to inform your spirit of this concerning you: He said that He has spoken it and will bring it to pass. He has purposed it and He also will do it in Jesus' mighty and precious name. Amen.

"In Jesus' mighty name this three-letter word BUT is of the devil and shall not pass through your mouth. You were made to be greater than your fathers and mothers, and all that were before you. There is nothing contrary about your sure future so long as you remain on the sure foundation which is Christ Jesus, the only wise god, and our Lord and Savior who is the author and finisher of your faith. In Jesus' name I pray. Amen."

CHAPTER 6

Praying for a Godly Marriage

Marriage was instituted by the Lord in the garden of Eden. Therefore, it is wise for married couples to keep the Lord in their marriages if they want to experience the entirety of the blessings of this divine union. After creating Adam, God realized something was missing. All the other animals had a male and a female, but not Adam. So, God says, it is not good that a man should be alone; I will make him a help meet for him (Genesis 2:18). In the Amplified translation it is written as this help meet being suitable, complementary, and adapted for the man. God made a woman from Adam's rib as a secondary creation. This was such a wonderful sight for Adam that he recited a poem! "This is now bone of my bones, and flesh of my flesh: she shall be called Woman, because she was taken out of Man." The word woman means a man with a womb, explaining the rest of Adam's poem. "Therefore shall a man leave his father and his mother, and shall cleave unto his wife: and they shall be one flesh" (Genesis 2:24).

My prayer for all husbands and single men seeking a wife is for God to open our eyes to view women as Adam did when God first made her. In Jesus' name. Amen.

I am not writing on this divine and precious topic to start a debate on who or what is responsible for today's high divorce rate. However, I can exercise my senses to see (Hebrews 5:14) that this institution established by God is being attacked by God relentlessly in these end times. Every married couple, whether their marriage is strong or wavering, need to be constantly praying for it along with the marriages of our other brothers and sisters in Christ.

Blessed be God, and our Lord Jesus Christ for His precious Spirit, who has moved me to be a part of the solution in strengthening our marriages. I sincerely believe in marriage between a man and a woman, I believe God honors and blesses it when it is based on his biblical guidelines, but I am not naïve of the hard work married couples must put forth to ensure they have a godly marriage. I believe that a husband and wife who will invest the time and effort to pray together will surely succeed in their marriage. Husbands and wives must conduct daily prayer sessions together at set times, even if it is not at a set location because there may be times they are not able to be in the same place at once.

Let us focus on the key to achieving a good and godly marriage. Jesus Christ is so wonderful because He is such a thoughtful teacher. He teaches us in Matthew 18:19, "Again I say unto you, that if two of you shall agree on earth as touching anything that they shall ask it, it shall be done for them of my Father which is in heaven."

When was the last time you touched your spouse's hands to agree in prayer? And if you have been obedient, then how often is your obedience? Are you consistent and persistent in prayer time together? Just remember, Satan is consistent and persistent in attacking our marriages. He never takes a vacation or a day off.

The power is in unity, and whenever two people agree in prayer, God must perform it in Jesus' name. Listen to me, beloved husbands and wives, your abilities and perfection lies in your ability to agree in prayer. "Can two walk together unless they have agreed to do so" (Amos 3:3)? The answer is no, it is impossible to walk together without agreeing to do so, and sadly, this is the root of most of our marital problems. I want to inform you that when the two of you make an effort to agree in prayer, you are basically making an appointment with divine success.

There is no anger too great to prevent a man and his wife from becoming prayer partners.

Solomon said in Ecclesiastes 3:9 that two are better than one, because they have a good reward for their labor. For if they fall, the one will lift up his fellow or partner: but WOE to him that is alone when he falls; for he has no one to help him up.

Yes, the reward is a good and godly marriage, and the labor here is both parties being diligent to pray together, no matter if you are angry at each other, or whose fault it is. Don't focus on petty matters, but strive to maintain what God Himself has put together. Achieving a good and godly marriage takes spiritual efforts, which consist of praying and agreeing spiritually. Yes, we can all agree on things in the flesh, but those things are temporal. What is done in the spirit is eternal; this agreement is honored by God. Husbands, if you love your wives, love them by reaching out to them and grabbing their hands, nurturing them in daily prayer sessions and bible studies. Trust me, I can relate to the difficulties which comes with this spiritual effort, but God trusted you when He made you the Head of the woman. Wives, if you love your husbands, show it by respecting them due to your submission in all humility. Welcome their prayer efforts and spiritual subjections to God. Don't break them down, instead build them up.

The bible says in Proverbs 14:1, "The wise woman builds her house, but the foolish tears it down with her own hands." I encourage you, husbands and wives, to be diligent in these teachings. If you will, then in about a month, godly living will become the norm in your relationship. I promise, you will see and feel the manifestation of God's glory upon your marriage.

To summarize this entire chapter in a couple of words, I would say to both of you, God must be the third person in your marriage who is first in all activities.

Remember this my beloved married couples, and those who are going into marriage, a cord of three strands is not easily or quickly broken (Ecclesiastes 4:12).

God Himself established marriage, and when it is affected, God is affected. In Genesis 39:9, before Joseph fled from Potiphar's wife, he replied to her that he cannot do such great wickedness and sin against God. When our marriages are attacked, God feels the pain more than we do. We must join together to pray diligently for all marriages to prosper. Marriage is the only thing that causes two people to become one, and only God can oversee this great union.

Good News Translation: "No human being must separate what God has joined together."

Message Translation: "Because God created this organic union of the two sexes, no one should desecrate his art by cutting them apart."

New Century Translation: "God has joined the two together, so no one should separate them."

I charge all husbands and wives in every village, town, city, and nations to join with me in one accord in praying for all marriages.

The following prayer point should be prayed together by spouses daily.

"Night and day praying exceedingly that we might see your face, and might perfect that which is lacking in your faith." (1 Thessalonians 3:10)

Prayer point: "Father God, I pray that you might perfect all that is lacking in our faith that is discouraging our hope of a prosperous marriage. In Jesus' name. Amen."

"But it is good to be zealously affected always in good thing, and not only when I am present with you." (Galatians 4:18)

Prayer point: "Lord, help to be a good husband or wife, and to love my spouse, especially when they are not present."

"He that loves not knows not God, for God is Love." (1 John 4:18)

Prayer point: "Father God, teach us to how to love one another in our marriage like you love us through your Son Jesus Christ. In Jesus' name. Amen."

"He will fulfill the desire of them that fear him: He also will hear their cry, and will save them." (Psalm 145:19)

Prayer point: "Lord, I pray that you will fulfill our desire to make our marriage work. Lord, also hear all our prayers concerning our marriage, and save it from all attacks of Satan. In Jesus' name. Amen."

"Grace and peace be multiplied unto you through the knowledge of God, and of Jesus our Lord." (2 Peter 1:1)

Prayer point: "Lord, may you always multiply your grace and peace upon our marriage. In Jesus' name. Amen."

"Thou shalt hide them in the secret of thy presence from the plot of men; you keep them secretly in Your shelter from the strife of tongues." (Psalm 31:20)

Prayer point: "Lord Jesus, hide our marriage in Your secret presence and under Your secret shelter from the conspiracies of people who wish evil upon it. In Jesus' name. Amen."

"Many are the sorrows of the wicked, but he who trusts in the Lord, Loving-kindness shall surround him. (Psalm 32:10)

Prayer point: "Father God, we pray that You would increase our trust in You, so that Your loving kindness can surround our marriage always. In Jesus' name. Amen."

"A quarrelsome or contentious wife is like a constant dripping on a rainy day." (Proverbs 27:15)

Prayer point: "Lord, I know that many of the reasons our marriage is going bad is because of my attitude towards my husband. Please help me to get control over my anger and to speak grace unto him. Take this contentious spirit from me O Lord, so I can become the wife you have created me to be. In Jesus' name. Amen."

"God be merciful unto us, and bless us, and cause His face to shine upon us." (Psalm 67:1)

Prayer point: "Lord, my wife and I have come before you to ask for your mercy upon our marriage, and to bless the works of Your hand. Lord God, cause Your precious face to shine upon our union. In Jesus' name. Amen."

"If I regard iniquity in my heart, the Lord will not hear me." (Psalm 66:18)

Prayer point: "Lord God, one of the problems in our marriage is that we hold grudges in our hearts after a fight. Help my wife and I to quickly forgive one another after every altercation and disagreement. In Jesus' name. Amen."

"Let my prosecutors be put to shame, but keep me from shame. Let them be terrified, but keep me from terror. Bring on them the day of disaster and destroy them with double destruction." (Jeremiah 17:18)

Prayer point: "Father, in the name of Jesus Christ, let every demonic agent assigned to our marriage be destroyed with double destruction. In Jesus' name. Amen."

"And thou shalt speak unto him, and put words in his mouth: and I will be with thy mouth, and with his mouth, and will teach you what you shall do." (Exodus 4:15)

Prayer point: "Lord, be with our mouth in this marriage. Put words of edification in our mouths during times of altercation so that we do not say things which will lead to regret later on. In Jesus' name. Amen."

"And let the beauty of the Lord our God be upon us; and establish thou the work of our hands upon us; yea, the work of our hands establish thou it." (Psalm 90:17)

Prayer point: "Father God, we pray always to you for Your beauty to rest upon our marriage, and that You, O Lord, will establish the works of our hand in this marriage. In Jesus' name. Amen."

"He must increase, but we must decrease." (John 3:30)

Prayer point: "Lord, help us to always humble ourselves before You in this marriage and to decrease in self, so You, O Lord, and your precious Holy spirit can increase mightily in our marriage. In Jesus' name. Amen."

"That the name of our Lord Jesus Christ may be glorified in you and you in Him, according to the grace of our God and the Lord Jesus Christ." (2 Thessalonians 1:12)

Prayer point: "Lord Jesus, may Your Holy name always be glorified in our marriage. In Jesus' name. Amen."

"And may the Lord cause you to increase and abound in love for one another, and for all people, just as we also do for you." (1 Thessalonians 4:12)

Prayer point: "Lord, make us to increase and abound in Your unconditional towards one another in our marriage. In Jesus' name. Amen."

"And David went on, and grew great, and the Lord God of hosts was with him." (2 Samuel 5:10)

Prayer point: "Lord, I pray for Your help to make our marriage to grow great. In Jesus' name. Amen."

"Now the Lord is that spirit: and where the spirit of the Lord is, there is liberty." (2 Corinthians 3:17)

Prayer point: "Father God, may our marriage abide in the comfort and liberty of Your Holy Spirit. In Jesus' name. Amen."

"So Gideon said to Him, 'if I have found favor in your sight, then show me a sign that it is You who speak with me.'" (Judges 6:17)

Prayer point: "Lord Jesus, if you are truly in favor of the fruitfulness of our marriage, show us a sign that You are with us in our efforts. In Jesus' name. Amen."

"And you will also decree a thing, and it will be established for you." (Job 22:28)

Prayer point: "Lord, my spouse and I are standing humbly before you because Your word said that we shall decree a thing, and it shall be established for us. Lord, together we decree your goodness, Your peace, Your presence, Your guidance, Your faithfulness, Your blessings, Your anointing, and Your uncommon favor upon our marriage. In Jesus' mighty name we pray. Amen."

"For if there be first a willing mind, it is accepted according to that a man has, and not according to that he has not." (2 Corinthians 8:12)

Prayer point: "Father God, give my spouse and me a willing mind to walk together, pray together, dance together, talk together, and to put forth a diligent effort to prosper in our marriage. In Jesus' name. Amen."

"Wives, submit yourselves unto your own husband, as it is fit in the Lord." (Colossians 3:18)

Prayer point: "Lord, I know You created me for obedience, so help me express this to my husband, and to totally submit myself to him. In Jesus' name. Amen."

"Husbands, love your wives, and be not bitter against them." (Colossians 3:19)

Prayer point: "Father God, help me to truly love my wife, and to cease from holding petty grudges in my heart towards her, especially when she has wronged me. In Jesus' name. Amen."

CHAPTER 7

Personal Growth in the Lord

There is no limit on one's maturity in Christ. Paul says that there are deeper depths and higher heights to attain in Christ Jesus. Apostle Paul also said in 1 Timothy 4:8 that "bodily exercise profits little, but godliness is profitable unto all things, having the promise of the life that is now, and that which to come." This is why Peter encourages us to give all diligence to add to our faith virtue, and to virtue knowledge; and to knowledge temperance, and to temperance patience, and to patience godliness, and to godliness brotherly kindness, and to brotherly kindness charity or love (1 Peter 1:5-7).

There is an urgent need for Gods people to continue to grow spiritually in Him. There is no such thing as having enough of Christ Jesus. The Lord is telling you to quench not the spirit, and to pray without ceasing, and earnestly desire spiritual gifts more than ever before, because He is willing to lavish them upon His beloved children in these final hours.

There is something priceless and precious about knowing God deeper, and we see this clearly in the ministry of two great men of God. Moses was a man who parted the Red Sea due to the power of God. He was a man who called down manna from heaven and ate with God, but he still had an earnest desire to know God. "Now therefore, I pray thee, If I have found grace in thy sight, show me now thy way, **that I may know thee** that I may find grace in thy sight, and consider that this nation is thy people" (Exodus 33:13). Being used by God to do all those miracles in Egypt then seeing God face to face when He wrote the Ten Commandments was still not enough for Moses. He desired even more knowledge, more presence, more spirit, and a greater intimacy with God.

Now let us look at the Apostle Paul, a man God delivered from the works of Satan, a man who God showed mysteries, and wrote the majority of the New Testament. This same Paul was given the Gospel of the grace of God, which we preach to the world in this dispensation. For three years, Paul received one on one instruction from Jesus while he was in Arabia (Galatians 1:12, 17-18). Paul was the Apostle to the Gentiles (Romans 11:13), and those of us who are saved today are the fruit of Paul's ministry. This same Paul farther explained the gospel to the other disciples, who also brought the back the dead to life. Despite all of these accomplishments, he was not satisfied with all that he had experienced. He expressed this hunger and desire in Philippians 3:10. "I want to know Christ and the power of his resurrection and the fellowship of his sufferings, becoming like him in his death, and so somehow, to attain to the resurrection of the dead."

These two great men were truly on fire for God and the Lord Jesus, and we are called to have this same hunger; to grow in the knowledge of God, and to remain on fire for Him until His glorious appearing. Our God is a consuming fire, so why should he settle for a lukewarm child of God?

There are five levels of knowing a thing. I am going to use President Barack Obama as an example to express these five levels.

1. Distant knowledge- This is not a personal knowledge, it is being aware of the existence of a person. We know Barack Obama was the president because we saw him on television and heard him on other media.

2. Casual knowledge- This knowledge is obtained by people who have some type of interaction with a person, no matter how small. These would be the various aides who worked in his administration in some capacity where they might have had the opportunity to get a glimpse of him in person.

3. Relative Knowledge- This is knowledge that goes beyond the immediate and knows a person in areas outside of their official capacity. These would be the people who grew up with President Obama such us his family or fellow students in college. They would have a different perspective than those with casual knowledge because they will have seen him outside of his being "on the job."

4. Father to son knowledge- This knowledge can only be obtained by President Obama's children. His two girls know him in a special private intimate way that no one else can do. This is one of the privileges of having him for a father.

5. Conjugal- This is the fifth and most intimate level of knowing a thing- it is defined as the process of joining with the person to become one. In President Obama's life, this is reserved for one person, his wife, Mrs. Barack Obama. While the President may share a great deal of things with the media, co-workers, friends, even his daughters, but the only one who hears the deep secrets in secret places is his blessed wife. This is the level which God calls us to operate on every day of our lives. The bible says in Ephesians 5:31-32, "For this cause shall a man leave his father and mother, and shall be joined unto his wife, and they two shall be one flesh. This is a great mystery, but I speak concerning Christ and the church."

Ladies, and gentlemen, we are the church, the body of Christ. Praise the Lord! Real and intimate knowledge is what you are driven to learn more of. Many people know about God, but they do not really know God, nor do they approach the level of intimacy God desires from His beloved children. Both Moses and Paul expressed their yearning to obtain this level of intimacy when they cried out, saying that they wanted to know God. "To know," in Hebrew is YADA, which means to have intimacy in the context of a sexual relationship. You ask, why does God want us to have such an experience with Him? The word of God says in Isaiah 54:5, "For thy Maker is thine husband; the Lord of hosts is his name; and thy Redeemer the Holy one of Israel; the God of the whole earth shall he be called." Hallelujah somebody!

Brothers and sisters in Christ, this is not the time to settle for a distant, casual relationship and Father to son knowledge of God. Instead, all of our focus should be on knowing God on the conjugal level. He commanded us in Deuteronomy 6:5 to love God with all our heart, with all our souls, and with all our might. I remember many times when even my close friends called me a fanatic because of my love and zeal for God and His words. My immediate response would be, "Yes I am His #1 fan." I encourage you to not allow anyone, including demons, to discourage your zeal to love God, and to know Him more and more.

The sad reality is, not everyone in the body of Christ truly loves God, but just as the foolish virgins were exposed, so will these people be exposed when Jesus returns. Individually, we must increase our love and desire to seek the Lord daily.

It is a personal decision for a person to want to know God more. The bible says in Luke 10:1 that there were 70 disciples, and out of these 70, the bible tells us in Mark 3:14 that the number was decreased to twelve disciples, whom he called apostles. Then we find out in Luke 9:28, that out of these twelve, only three, Peter, John, and James were chosen by the Lord to accompany him to the Mount of Transfiguration. But out of all the disciples, there was only one, John, who was closer to Jesus than any other person. John was operating on this conjugal level; an intimate level. "Now there was leaning on Jesus' bosom one of his disciples, whom Jesus loved" (John 13:23). God is looking for disciples who love Him so much that their hunger to know Him leads them to lay on His bosom. This is where secrets are shared and questions are answered. This where fresh revelations are revealed, and where personal growth is sustained and preserved. Come closer to God and He will always be near you. Desire to know Him more and more, and may your spiritual cup overflow eternally. The Lord wants me to let you know that the day of His returning is coming very near, and to those who say, "I used to be on fire but I'm not anymore. I know I should get on fire and continue to burn more than ever for God's sake," I want to ask, "what are you waiting for?" The Lord is saying to you today, to call to remembrance your former days when you first accepted Christ and were on fire.

"Blessed, happy, fortunate, and to be envied are those servants whom the master finds awake and alert and watching when he comes. Truly I say to you, he will gird himself and have them recline at table and will come and serve them. Whether he comes in the second watch, or even in the third, and finds them so, blessed are those servants. But understand this; if the owner of the house had known at what hour the thief was coming, he would not have let his house be broken into. You also must be ready, because the Son of Man will come at an hour when you do not expect him." (Luke 12:37-40)

The purpose of this chapter is to keep your fire blazing for Jesus forevermore. These following prayer points will help your personal growth in the Lord and help restart your spiritual engine. I say get on fire and continue to burn for Jesus Christ.

"And of the angels he said, who makes his angels spirits, and his ministers or servants a flame of fire." (Hebrews 1:17)

Prayer point: "Father God, set me ablaze, set me on fire, and flame me up in Jesus' mighty name. Amen."

"Blessed are they which do hunger and thirst after righteousness; for they shall be filled." (Matthew 5:5)

Prayer point: "Lord God, I pray that You will increase my hunger and thirst for Your word, work, righteousness, holiness, and for only heavenly things. In Jesus' name. Amen."

"But You have exalted my horn like that of the wild ox. I have been anointed with fresh oil." (Psalm 92:10)

Prayer points: "Anoint me O Lord with fresh oil, and bless me with a fresh anointing. In Jesus' name. Amen."

"And as they began to speak, the Holy Ghost fell on them, as on us at the beginning." (Acts 11:15)

Prayer point: "Lord, may Your Holy Spirit fall spontaneously upon me everywhere I go. In Jesus' name. Amen."

"They go from strength to strength, every one of them in Zion appears before God." (Psalm 84:7)

Prayer point: "Father God, may I always go from strength to strength on this great journey. In Jesus' name. Amen."

"And all the people were trying to touch Him, for power was coming from Him and healing them all." (Luke 6:19)

Prayer point: "Lord, I pray that all people will be healed from Your healing within me. In Jesus' precious name. Amen."

"But he passing through the midst of them went his way." (Luke 4:30)

Prayer point: "Lord God, bless me with the anointing to pass through my enemies whenever they come to threaten my life. In Jesus' name. Amen."

"But when they failed to find them, they dragged Jason and some brethren before the city authorities, crying. These men who turned the world UPSIDE down have come here also." (Acts 17:6)

Prayer point: "Lord, give me the anointing to turn this world upside down with Your gospel. In Jesus' name. Amen."

"You have no part or portion in this matter; for thy heart is not right in the sight of God." (Acts 8:21)

Prayer point: "Lord, make my heart to be right in Your sight always. In Jesus' name. Amen."

"But Saul increase the more in strength, and confounded the Jews which dwell at Damascus, proving that this is Jesus is the Christ." (Acts 9:22)

Prayer point: "Lord, may I continue to increase in strength for the sake of Your great name. In Jesus' name. Amen."

"For we walk by faith, and not by sight." (2 Corinthians 5:7)

Prayer point: "Father God, help me to live my life having full faith in You, and not to focus only on what is visible, but on the unseen certainties. In Jesus' name. Amen."

"Set your affection on things above, not on things on the earth." (Colossians 3:2)

Prayer point: "Lord, help me to look upon heavenly things and not earthy affairs. In Jesus' name. Amen."

"Everyone must do just as he has purposed in his heart, let he give, not grudgingly or under compulsion, for God loves a cheerful giver." (2 Corinthians 9:7)

Prayer point: "Lord, help me to be at peace when deciding to give; whether it is to You or to others in need. Let me give with a cheerful heart. Amen."

"Iron sharpens iron, so a man sharpens his friend." (Proverbs 27:17)

Prayer point: "Lord, send me a good friend in Christ to help sharpen my spiritual life daily. In Jesus' name. Amen."

"Who are you to judge the servant of another? To his own master he stands or falls; and he will stand, for the Lord is able to make him stand." (Romans 14:4)

Prayer point: "Father God, make me to stand in my weakness, especially when I fall short of Your glory. Amen."

"But you, why do you judge your brother? Or you again, why do you regard your brother with contempt? For we will all stand before the judgment seat of God." (Romans 14:10)

Prayer point: "Heavenly Father, I pray that You would remove this judging spirit from my heart and teach me to always encourage others who are not living according to Your standards. In Jesus' name. Amen."

"For I long to see you, that I may impart unto you some spiritual gift, to the end that you may be established." (Romans 1:11)

Prayer point: "Lord, I pray that You would impart unto me spiritual gifts. I desire the gift of healing, speaking in tongues, word of knowledge, wisdom, prophesy, gift of interpretation, and discerning of dreams. In Jesus' name. Amen."

"And when they had prayed, the place was shaken where they were assembled together, and they were filled with the Holy Ghost, and they spoke the word of God with boldness." (Acts 4:31)

Prayer point: "Father God, I pray for Your power to be upon my prayers, so that every time I pray, Satan's kingdom and his plans shall shake and suffer a mighty defeat. In Jesus' name. Amen."

"And when they were come, and had gathered the church together, they rehearsed all that God had done with them, and how he had opened the door of faith unto the gentiles." (Acts 14:27)

Prayer point: "Lord, help me to think about the things that You do for me daily. I pray that the door of faith will be open unto me. In Jesus' name. Amen."

"And God wrought special miracles by the hands of Paul." (Acts 19:11)

Prayer point: "Lord, just as you worked special, unusual, and extraordinary miracles at the hands of Your servant Paul, so shall You O Lord do unto me. In Jesus' mighty name. Amen."

"Show me thy ways, O Lord; teach me thy paths. Lead me in thy truth, teach me; for thou art the God of my salvation; on thee do I wait all the day." (Psalm 25:4, 5)

Prayer point: "Father God, show me your ways, for mine is wrong. Teach me Your path, for mine is crooked, and lead me in thy truth, for my life is filled with all lies. Teach me Jesus and I will always wait for Your salvation. In Jesus' name I pray. Amen."

"I will instruct thee and teach thee in the way which thou shalt go; I will guide you with mine eye."

Prayer point: "Lord God, instruct and teach my every movement. Guide my going and coming with Your eye. In Jesus' name. Amen."

"For God maketh my heart soft, and the Almighty troubled me." (Job 23:16)

Prayer point: "Lord, let my heart be melted before You. May I be terrified before You in reverence of You. In Jesus' name. Amen."

"And David inquired at the Lord, saying, Shall I pursue after this troop? Shall I overtake them? And Him answered him, pursue: for thou shall surely overtake them, and without fail recover all." (1 Samuel 30:8)

Prayer point: "Lord, may Your spirit remind me to always inquire of Your Divine input or confirmation in my time of distress. In Jesus' name. Amen."

"The large crowd of the Jews then learned that He was there; and they came, not for Jesus sake only, but that they might also see Lazarus, whom He raised from the dead." (John 12:9)

Prayer point: "Father God, I pray that countless people will come to You because of what You have done in my life. May my testimony draw people to Jesus Christ. In Jesus' name. Amen."

"And they were astonished at his doctrine; for his word was with power." (Luke 4:32)

Prayer point: "O Lord God, I pray that people from every nation will stand in amazement of my teaching of Your word, and that Your words will come forth from my lips with power in the name of Jesus Christ of Nazareth. In Jesus' name. Amen."

"How sweet are thy words unto my taste! Yea sweeter than honey to my mouth." (Psalm 119:103)

Prayer point: "Father God, may Your words leave a sweet taste in my mouth each time I try to read my bible, so my love for Your word can grow in me. In Jesus' name. Amen."

"Open thou mine eyes, that I may behold wondrous things out of thy law. (Psalm 119:18)

Prayer point: "Lord, open my spiritual eyes to see and comprehend wonderful things out of Your word. In Jesus' name. Amen."

"I have even heard of thee, that the spirit of the gods in thee, and that light and understanding and excellent wisdom is found in thee." (Daniel 5:12, 14)

Prayer point: "Lord, may Your spirit be recognized in and upon me everywhere I go. Let light, understanding, excellent wisdom, excellent spirit, knowledge, and interpretation of dreams be found in me. In Jesus' name. Amen."

"Therefore if God gave to them the same gift as He gave to us also after believing in the Lord Jesus Christ, who was I that I could stand in God's way?" (Acts 11:17)

Prayer point: "Father God, whatever I am currently or have been doing to stand in the way of You reaching me, I pray that Your Holy Ghost fire shall expose and consume it immediately. In the name of Jesus. Amen."

"Rooted and built up in Him, and established in the faith, as you have been taught, abounding therefore with thanksgiving." (Colossians 2:7)

Prayer point: "Lord, help me to be rooted and built up in You, and to be established in faith, and to overflow with gratitude due to Your grace upon my life. In Jesus' name. Amen."

"And all the people were trying to touch Him, for power was coming from Him and healing them all." (Luke 6:19)

Prayer point: "Lord Jesus, Your word says, 'greater works will we do than this,' and Your word also says 'that we have not because we ask not.' Therefore, I am praying that power shall come forth from within me to heal Your beloved people in this generation. In Jesus' name. Amen."

"Your commandments make me wiser than my enemies, for they are ever with me." (Psalm 119:98)

Prayer point: "Lord, may Your word make me wiser than all my enemies. In Jesus' name. Amen."

"Thus says the Lord, Heaven is my throne and earth is my footstool. Where is a house you could build for Me? And where is the place of My rest? For my hands made all these things, all these things came to being because of Me. But to this one I will look, to him who is humble and contrite of spirit, and who trembles at My word." (Isaiah 66:1, 2)

Prayer point: "Lord, continue to work on me, for my heart desire is to be Your dwelling place and Your place of rest. Create in me a humble and broken spirit O LORD, the kind that trembles at the sight of Your word. In Jesus' name. Amen."

CHAPTER 8

Prayers for the Loss of Loved Ones

Hebrews 9:27 confirms to us that man is destined to die once, and after that face judgment. However, there are three different deaths referred to in scripture.

1. Spiritual death- a complete disconnection from God while living on earth.
2. Physical Death- this is the death Hebrews 9:27 is referring to, it is the one we will all experience one day as it pleases our Creator, if the Lord tarries.
3. Eternal Death- this death takes place after the Great White Throne Judgment. Those whose names are not found in the Lamb's book of life because, while they were alive physically, they refused to accept Christ as Lord and Savior, will be cast into the Lake of Fire where they will spend eternity.

Our focus in this sensitive, but practical and realistic chapter is to examine the pain of losing a loved one to death's embrace. This is a difficult time for people of every color, tribe, religion, or nationality. Losing a loved one was, and still is, a difficult time for our Savior Jesus Christ, who, after receiving the news of His friend Lazarus' death, went to where he was laid. The bible says in John 11:32 that "Jesus wept," meaning He expressed grief, sorrow, and displayed an overpowering level of emotion over the loss of His friend.

My brothers and sisters, we do not have to go through this difficult time alone. We have a Master who can relate to the distress of losing a loved one.

I want to help encourage you in your time of mourning by directing you to the word of God. The bible is the only book where the Author knows every need of His readers beforehand. So if we are seeking comfort during these difficult times, the word of God is a great place to look!

"The righteous perish, and no man takes it to heart, and merciful men are taken away from the evil to come. He shall enter into peace: they shall rest in their beds, each one walking in his uprightness." (Isaiah 57:1, 2)

To all those who may be grieving from the loss of a loved one, be encouraged by what the word of God is saying to you in your time of need. If your loved one has trusted Jesus as their Lord and Savior, they have gone to a better place, a place where God shall wipe away all tears forever. A place with no more pain or death. Your son, daughter, father, mother, grandmother, grandfather, uncle, aunt, cousin, teacher, friend, or mentor, who has called upon Christ as their Lord and Savior has entered into a place of peace in His presence. Your loved one is resting with everlasting joy while smiling down upon you in excitement of your righteous outcome.

I want to say to you right now, that I am so sorry about your loss, and I stand with you in the spirit as you attempt to find comfort by praying the following scriptural prayer points.

I want to also encourage you by informing you that my wife, Victorious, and I, lost a week-old baby boy named Matthias Elisha Gbeintor. We were able to be strong and unmoved during our experience because we used the word of God as written in this chapter each and every day to carry us through this dark valley. I encourage you to do the same.

"They that sow in tears shall reap in joy." (Psalm 126:5)

Prayer point: "Lord God, may abundant joy be granted unto me and my family. In Jesus' name. Amen."

"And God remembered Noah, and every living thing, and all the cattle that was with him in the ark; and God made a wind to pass over the earth, and the waters assuaged." (Genesis 8:1)

Prayer point: "Lord, remember me, my family, friends, job, heart, and my thoughts in this difficult time. In Jesus' name. Amen."

"May the Lord answer you in the day of trouble." (Psalm 20:1)

Prayer point: "Lord, your word says that You will answer us in our time of distress. We are holding you firm to Your word. In Jesus' name. Amen.

"In the day when I cried thou answered me, and strengthen me with strength in my soul." (Psalm 138:3)

Prayer point: "Father God, strengthen our souls and make us to be bold. In Jesus' name. Amen."

"As the mountains surround Jerusalem, so the Lord surrounds His people from this time forth and forever." (Psalm 125:3)

Prayer point: "We need you to surround our family O Lord, like the mountains of Jerusalem, now and always. In Jesus' mighty name. Amen."

"My voice shalt thou hear in the morning will I direct my prayer unto thee, and will look up." (Psalm 5:3)

Prayer point- "Lord Jesus, as we are directing all of our prayers unto thee during our time of need, help us to continue to look up to You O Lord for our comfort. In Jesus' name. Amen."

"But thou, O Lord, art a shield for me; my glory, and the lifter up of mine head." (Psalm 3:3)

Prayer point: "Lord, continue to shield us in this time of mourning, and may you continue to lift the heads of those who are not able to bear their sorrow. In Jesus' name. Amen."

"Many are the afflictions of the righteous; but the Lord delivereth him out of them all." (Psalm 34:19)

Prayer point: "Lord Jesus, may You deliver us out of our present afflictions. In Jesus' name. Amen."

"Thou shalt increase my greatness, and comfort me on every side." (Psalm 71:21)

Prayer point: "Lord, may Your Holy Spirit comfort our families on every side in our time of distress. In Jesus' name. Amen."

"And it shall come to pass in the day that the Lord shall give thee rest from thy sorrow, and from thy fear, and from the hard bondage wherein thou wast made to serve." (Isaiah 14:3)

Prayer point: "Lord Jesus, give us rest from all fears of moving forward, and the hard times which accompany losing a loved one. In Jesus' name. Amen."

"And, behold, the glory of the God of Israel came from the way of the east: and his voice was like a noise of many waters: and the earth shined with His glory." (Ezekiel 43:2)

Prayer point: "Father God, may you cause Your glory to shine upon our loved ones as we experience this time of mourning. In Jesus' name. Amen."

CHAPTER 9

Prayers for Our Children

They say, "it takes a village to raise a child," but I say "that it takes that same village to pray for our children." Notice I keep saying our children, this is because when it comes to children, everyone should stand together on this sensitive topic. We are all a living testimony of the prayers of our parents or others who were led to actively keep us in their prayers and have a godly influence in our lives. Children are the number one target of the devil and his demons here on earth because children are an heritage of the Lord (Psalm 127:3-5). He also goes after children because he knows they are so innocent and trusting. They have a natural tendency to trust those in authority, and the devil knows he can use this simple trust to bring harmful things into their lives and minds.

We are here today because of children who were born and blessed from previous generations. If the devil and his demons can poison our children, then he will have succeeded in killing our blessings which come from God. Satan and his forces are working overtime to make sure our children are not raised to be godly. "Now the sons of Eli were sons of Belial; they knew not the Lord (1 Samuel 2:12). Can you imagine being a pastor and having your children failing in school, fighting, drinking, smoking, having sex with all the church ladies, not attending church services, or no longer reading the bible. This was the situation Eli the priest was faced with. The word Belial in the Hebrew language means worthless, good for nothing, wicked, ruin, unprofitable, base fellow. This is Satan's desire for our children, and I rebuke it right now in the mighty Jesus Christ. The Lord handpicked these following scriptures, and prayer points to be prayed over our children daily.

"Now the sons Eli were sons of Belial; they knew not the Lord." (1 Samuel 2:12)

Prayer point: "Father God, I overturn the curse of Belial, good for nothing, spirit of worthlessness, destructive spirit of ruin from my children's children from generation to generation. In Jesus' mighty name. Amen."

"But Samuel ministered before the Lord, being a child, girded with linen ephod." (1 Samuel 2:18)

Prayer point: "Lord, grant my children the grace to minister or serve in the church before you all the days of their lives. In Jesus' name. Amen.

"And he said unto them, why do ye such things: for I hear of your evil dealings by all this people." (1 Samuel 2:23-24)

Prayer point: "Lord, may my children's actions cause no evil report to come into my ears. May I hear only good reports from the community about them. May my children's behavior cause many to be encouraged and not discouraged. In Jesus' name. Amen."

"And the child Samuel grew on, and was favored both with the Lord, and with men." (1 Samuel 2:26)

Prayer point: "Lord Jesus, may my children grow in favor with you and everyone they may encounter in life. In Jesus' name. Amen."

"And the child grew, and waxed strong in spirit, filled with wisdom; and the grace of God was upon him." (Luke 2:40)

Prayer point: "Father God, may You strengthen my children with Your Spirit. Lavish Your wisdom upon them, and may Your grace escort them every step You order for them in life. In Jesus' name. Amen."

"Mine eyes are ever toward the Lord; for he shall pluck my feet out the net." (Psalm 25:15)

Prayer point: "Father God, keep the eyes of my children towards You, so that they may be kept from every entanglement of Satan. In Jesus' mighty name. Amen."

"Whosoever keepeth the law is a wise son; but he that is a companion of riotous men shameth his father." (Proverbs 28:7)

Prayer point- "Lord, may my children be obedient to Your word, especially when they are around ungodly children and people. In Jesus' name. Amen."

"I rejoiced greatly that I found of thy children walking in truth, as we have received a commandment from the Father." (2 John 1:4)

Prayer point: "Lord, I destroy the curse of lying upon my children's lives. May they be found always walking in Your truth. I delete every lying spirit inherited from their bloodline. In Jesus' name. Amen."

"And many of the children of Israel shall He turn to their God." (Luke 1:16)

Prayer point- "Father God, may you cause my children to turn to You whenever they are heading on a path which does not please You. In Jesus' name. Amen."

"I shall not die, but live, and declare the works of the Lord." (Psalm 118:17)

Prayer point: "I cancel and overturn the spirit of premature death from my children so that my children will live long and do the work of God powerfully. In Jesus' mighty name. Amen."

"As for these four children, God gave them knowledge and skill in all learning and wisdom: and Daniel had understanding in all visons and dreams." (Daniel 1:17)

Prayer point: "Lord of heaven and earth, giver of all knowledge and wisdom; may Your divine knowledge, skills, and wisdom be upon my children. Distinguish them from the rest of the world. In Jesus' name. Amen."

"Set a watch, O Lord, before my mouth; keep the door of my lips." (Psalm 141:3)

Prayer point: "Lord, may only blessings be spoken from the mouths of my children. Keep their lips from speaking cursings. In Jesus' name. Amen."

CHAPTER 10
Praying for Spiritual Events

Just like the world keeps its people busy with activities, we, the body of Christ, must find spiritual activities to keep the saints busy. I always say to my church family that they are either working for God or the devil.

One truth we need to remember about Satan is that, unlike God, he is not omnipresent, meaning he is not capable of being present in all places at all times. Because of this, he must use other means to obtain information or be a part of anything. He does this by delegating his authority to his demonic agents to spy, interrupt, or destroy spiritual gatherings of the saints. Satan walks to and fro throughout the whole earth and up and down in it, looking to devour people who are worshipping God at spiritual gatherings of any sort.

The reason I am passionate about this chapter is because I believe in the power of prayer before a spiritual event such as a church fundraiser, revival, memorial, funeral, wedding ceremony, baptism, ordinations, gospel musical programs, etc. They all have one thing in common, God is to be glorified in every event planned for His glory. I encourage you to take the time to put together a spiritual or church event prayer team who will meet weekly to pray these anointed prayer points on behalf of whatever events have been planned. From my experience, I can promise you, by God's grace, that the gates of hell shall not prevail upon whatever you are planning to do for the Lord's work. The Spirit of the Living God will be evoked in your programs mightily to bring forth the kind of results worthy of the Lord's glory. In Jesus' name. Amen.

"And that because of false brethren unawares brought in, who came in privily to spy out our liberty which we have in Christ Jesus, that they might bring us into bondage:" (Galatians 2:4)

Prayer point: "Lord, Jesus, may every demonic agent creeping in unawares to disrupt our peace in this service be discomforted in the mighty name of Jesus. Amen."

"These six [things] doth the Lord hate: yea, seven [are] an abomination unto him:" (Proverbs 6:16)

Prayer Point: "Lord, may You suppress everything that you hate personally, and not allow it to surface in this program. In Jesus' mighty name. Amen."

"But the Jews which believed not, moved with envy, took unto them certain lewd fellows of the baser sort, and gathered a company, and set all the city on an uproar, and assaulted the house of Jason, and sought to bring them out to the people." (Acts 17:5)

Prayer point: "O Lord, may only those who believe in what we are doing for you show up. Let every envious spirit that seeks to block our blessing be themselves blocked. In Jesus' name. Amen."

"Hide me from the secret counsel of the wicked; from the insurrection of the workers of iniquity:" (Psalm 64:2)

Prayer Point: "Father God, may this program be hidden from every wicked tongue. As they speak curses, so shall blessing be manifested in this program. In Jesus' name Amen."

"And it shall come to pass in the last days, [that] the mountain of the Lord's house shall be established in the top of the mountains, and shall be exalted above the hills; and all nations shall flow unto it." (Isaiah 2:2)

Prayer point: "Father, may Your Spirit cause people from every walk of life to flow to this program in the name of Jesus. Amen."

"For I, saith the Lord, will be unto her a wall of fire round about, and will be the glory in the midst of her." (Zechariah 2:5)

Prayer point: "Lord, may you barricade everything concerning this event with the wall of your consuming fire. In Jesus' name. Amen.

"Then the spirit took me up, and I heard behind me a voice of a great rushing, [saying], Blessed [be] the glory of the Lord from his place." (Ezekiel 3:12)

Prayer point: "Father God, may your Holy Ghost enable us to experience Your glory at this event. In Jesus' name. Amen."

"So the spirit lifted me up, and took me away, and I went in bitterness, in the heat of my spirit; but the hand of the Lord was strong upon me." (Ezekiel 3:14)

Prayer point: "Lord Jesus, as we are preparing to seek your face at this event, lift us up to each other in Your spirit. Let your Spirit be strong upon this program. In Jesus' name. Amen."

"Be silent, O all flesh, before the Lord: for He is raised up out of His holy habitation." (Zechariah 2:13)

Prayer point: "By the authority of the God of peace, I command every demonic thing to stand still in silence on the day of this program. In the name of Jesus Christ. Amen."

"I was in the Spirit on the Lord's day, and heard behind me a great voice, as of a trumpet." (Revelation 1:10)

Prayer point: "Lord, may everything we do on the day of this program be done in Your spirit. May only your voice speak to us at this event. In Jesus' name. Amen."

"Howbeit certain men clave unto him, and believed: among the which was Dionysius the Areopagite, and woman named Damaris, and others with them." (Acts 17:34)

Prayer point: "Lord, may this program bring salvation to someone's heart. May you take this opportunity to convict the hearts of your people as they attend this program. In Jesus' name. Amen."

CHAPTER 11

Prayer for Loved Ones in Prison and the Criminal Justice System

A ministry friend once told me during the early stages of my ministry, "One of the challenges you will face is that God will always test you to see if you believe the sermons you preach. Shortly after you preach on a certain area, God will bring a trial into your life on that exact same thing. When that happens, you may be tempted to not preach on certain areas. As a man of God, you must preach what God lays on your heart, no matter what."

In those days, I would diligently study, and prepare teachings and sermons on a daily basis. The overall tone of my messages were geared towards encouraging people to immediately stand in the power of the Lord, especially when they were at their lowest state. Scriptures such as 2 Timothy 2:3, Revelation 2:10, and Proverbs 24:10 were fuel to inflame this warrior spirit the Lord had placed in me. I would set myself on fire and let people watch me burn.

I was on a spiritual high with no real experience on how to conduct myself as a good solider during the storms of life. I was an arrogant young Minister who thought he could handle anything. Little did I know that God was about to humble me in a mighty way to show me the truth of John 15:5, "Without me ye can do nothing," and John 3:30, "He must increase, but I must decrease."

One morning, I went to my mother's house which was being rented out. I received word that a drunken tenant had nearly burned the house down. When I arrived, the house was filled with smoke. I confronted the tenant, who had fallen asleep cooking eggs and hot dogs, about his negligence, letting him know he had endangered others living in the house.

As I began opening the doors and windows to clear out the smoke, I overheard him yelling on the phone, saying that his life was in danger. He repeatedly told the police dispatcher that I had a gun and was threatening to shoot him.

I was working as an armed security officer at the time, and was in possession of a handgun. Suddenly, a chill went through my body the likes of which I had never felt before as I heard this drunk make up this lie about me. In less than five minutes, I received a phone call from the police dispatcher, instructing me to step outside to speak with the officers.

As I stepped outside the door, I was immediately met with bright blinding lights, followed by a loud voice ordering me to get on the ground. As I laid down compliantly, making sure to not make any sudden movement, I knew that the enemy, the devil, had used this drunken man, who was angry at my confronting him, to create this chaotic scene. I was being falsely accused, and I knew there were no words to convince the police that this was all just a misunderstanding.

I was taken to the police station for processing. While the paperwork was being completed, for the first time in my life as a young minister, I experienced the comforting power of the Holy Spirit. I immediately began quoting Psalm 91 over and over again. I remember the police officers asking each other what I was saying! One officer answered, "I think he is praying!" All of the spiritual training I had been given by the Lord were being put to good use.

Soon after, the officer read the charges against me; aggravated assault, terroristic threat, and having a firearm without a permit. My bail was set at $45,000. In my mind, I knew of no one who loved me enough to bail me out, either with $45,000 or 10% of that amount, which was $4,500. The Holy Spirit comforted me to embrace the reality that, if I could not get anyone to bail me out within 30 minutes, I was going to be transported to the county jail.

My first two days and nights in jail were unbearable. I spent most of the time mulling over in my mind ways to find a solution to get out of here. On my third night, I had a dream where I was saw a bright light. As I looked at the light, in the center was the huge figure of a man. He was radiating light and had lights from all angles shooting from His body. He reached out with His hand and placed it on my chest. Then He spoke to me in a kindly voice, saying, "I will never leave you nor forsake you." He also told me that I would not leave the jail until the inmates acknowledged me as their pastor, and then I woke up with joy in my heart.

This third day, I felt powerful, for I was certain that the Prince of Peace, the Light of my Salvation, had just visited me in my distress to clarify why I was going through all this, and what I needed to do to get out of this mess. Immediately, I began to pray with the inmates, especially with those in my cell. I listened to their stories regarding some of the circumstances that led them to this point, then gave them bible references to look up and read.

I began hosting daily bible studies when I noticed that the Christian services were always being cancelled for various reasons. The Lord instructed me to write scriptures on cut-out pieces of paper to give to the inmates based on their area of need. The most popular verse I was instructed to hand out was Psalm 27:14 "Wait on the Lord; be of good courage, and he shall strengthen thine heart; wait, I say, on the Lord."

Inmates began seeking me out, and each time the Lord would give me a word concerning their situation. God began to work. I would see inmates I had been praying with get released by family members who hated them, while other inmates would go to court and come back with positive news. I was excited that God was working greatly, but seeing others leave while I remained in jail for something I did not do, saddened me greatly.

One day, while out in the court playing basketball, I noticed that various inmates were calling me Pastor Zimbabwe. I don't know who told them I was from this country, but I realized that this was not the time to inform them that I was actually from Liberia. What was important was that the inmates were acknowledging me as their Pastor. I rejoiced in my heart, and was humbled to see that the Lord took me through all this to show me the power of His word when used in our prayers. I was now a living witness of this wonder-working power in our real-life issues.

After twelve days of being in jail, I was suddenly released by family and ministry friends. After being released, I continued praying all those verses the Lord revealed to me while I was in jail, awaiting my trial date. When I went to court, all the charges against me were dropped and expunged from my record. They also returned my handgun. The Lord put me through all this to show me the power of His word mixed in our prayers during the worst of troubles.

Maybe you or a loved one has been falsely accused or are going through some issues with the criminal justice system. Perhaps you are being dragged through the prison system, locked up without bail, or are facing immigration problems with your deportation pending. Whatever it is, I want to encourage you to trust God's word to do the impossible.

This chapter will make miracles possible in your impossible situation. The Most High Judge of the earth is able to make a way where there is no way. When Jesus says yes, no prosecutor can say no. Our God is a Way Maker when there is no path to see. I saw God turn things around for me when the enemy tried to trap me in the prison system, and He is excited to do the same for you, your loved ones, children, friends, or anybody else you know, as you pray the prayer points in this chapter with them.

"Let my sentence come forth from thy presence; let thine eyes behold the things that are equal." (Psalm 17:2)

Prayer point: "Father God, may my justice, vindication, and decisions come from your righteous presence. May you see what is right in this case. In Jesus' name. Amen."

"Take hold of shield and buckler, and stand up for mine help." (Psalm 35:2)

Prayer point: "Lord, prepare thyself. Position yourself O God to help me. In Jesus' name. Amen."

"Lord, how long wilt thou look on? Rescue my soul from their destructions, my darling from the lions." (Psalm 35:17)

Prayer point: "Father God, how long will you sit there and allow evil prosecutions to ruin my life? May you prepare my rescue. In Jesus' name. Amen."

"Yea, they opened their mouth wide against me, and said, Aha, aha, our eye hath seen it." (Psalm 35:21)

"This thou hast seen, O Lord: keep not silence: O Lord, be not far from me." (Psalm 35:22)

Prayer point: "Lord God, those who are using my time of distress to laugh and taunt me will also acknowledge and testify of your glory upon my life. In Jesus' name. Amen."

"And my tongue shall speak of thy righteousness and of thy praise all the day long." (Psalm 35:28)

Prayer point: "Father God, show up for me this time. My tongue will not rest speaking of your signs and wonders. In Jesus' name. Amen."

"They shall speak of the glory of thy kingdom, and talk of thy power;" (Psalm 145:11)

Prayer point: "Lord Jesus, may the display of your power in this court be the topic of all conversations. In Jesus' name. Amen."

"He will fulfil the desire of them that fear him: he also will hear their cry, and will save them." (Psalm 145:19)

Prayer point: "Lord, fill me with your righteous fear while I am going through this trial. In Jesus' name. Amen."

"He healeth the broken in heart, and bindeth up their wounds." (Psalm 147:3)

Prayer point: "Lord, people have hurt me so much that it consumes me. Ttake this time to heal and restore me. In Jesus' name. Amen."

"The Lord lifteth up the meek: he casteth the wicked down to the ground." (Psalm 147:6)

Prayer point: "Lord, develop in me the spirit of meekness in the midst of prosecution. In Jesus' name. Amen."

"Teach me thy way, O Lord, and lead me in a plain path, because of mine enemies." (Psalm 27:11)

Prayer point: "Lord, as I sit in this jail, teach me to walk right, and to reject the crooked way. In Jesus' name. Amen."

"Deliver me not over unto the will of mine enemies: for false witnesses are risen up against me, and such as breathe out cruelty." (Psalm 27:12)

Prayer point: "Father God, the devil desires to see evil rule my life, but do not place me into the evil intentions of the enemy. In Jesus' name. Amen."

"The Lord will give strength unto his people; the Lord will bless his people with peace." (Psalm 29:11)

Prayer point: "Lord, as my family member, friend, child, or spouse sits in prison in confusion, bless them with sudden peace. In Jesus' name. Amen."

"Wait on the Lord: be of good courage, and he shall strengthen thine heart: wait, I say, on the Lord." (Psalm 27:14)

Prayer point: "Lord God, develop in me the spiritual strength to wait on you during this court process. In Jesus' name. Amen."

"Thou hast turned for me my mourning into dancing: thou hast put off my sackcloth, and girded me with gladness;" (Psalm 30:11)

Prayer point: "Lord, I declare my season of turnaround in this court matter. In Jesus' name. Amen."

"Though I walk in the midst of trouble, thou wilt revive me: thou shalt stretch forth thine hand against the wrath of mine enemies, and thy right hand shall save me." (Psalm 138:7)

Prayer point: "Father God, I am in trouble. I am holding to your word to keep me from sinking lower. In Jesus' name. Amen."

"I will be glad and rejoice in thy mercy: for thou hast considered my trouble; thou hast known my soul in adversities;" (Psalm 31:7)

Prayer point: "Lord Jesus, look carefully and be attentive to me in my time of need. In Jesus' name. Amen."

"I am forgotten as a dead man out of mind: I am like a broken vessel." (Psalm 31:12)

"For I have heard the slander of many: fear was on every side: while they took counsel together against me, they devised to take away my life." (Psalm 31:13)

"But I trusted in thee, O Lord: I said, Thou art my God." (Psalm 31:14)

Prayer point: "Lord, no matter what hurt this experience may cause, I will trust you fully because you are my God of impossibilities. In Jesus' name. Amen."

CHAPTER 12
Ambush the Devil and His Demons

There is a West African song that says, "everyone's got their area." Whether this saying is grammatically correct or not, it is a true statement. What does this have to do with God? Simple, to let you know that God calls everyone to serve in different areas, but it is by the same Spirit.

On the topic of spiritual warfare, this is my area of interest and enjoyment. I believe this has a great deal to do with what my Grandmother told me while living in Liberia at the age of 7. In those days, I had one habit, to cause trouble in our village, and torment and kill snakes crawling from the nearby bush where we would gather for church services. I remember so vividly what my Grandmother boldly stated to me after I bashed two snakes with a piece of wood. She said, "All of the children in your age group are running away from snakes, but you are always so eager to pursue them and kill them without a second thought."

Then she followed by saying, "I believe that God has chosen you to one day be a thorn in Satan's work on earth." My Grandmother did not know how to speak English, but she had a bible that had been translated into our native dialect that she read constantly. She raised me and took me to church every day in our village. God spoke through her to me at that tender age to confirm my calling, which is to operate in the authority of the name of Jesus Christ to battle the works of darkness in my generation, and to teach believers how to effectively engage in spiritual warfare. I am the Joshua of my generation, and I am very proud to be a warrior for Christ. My intention in life, and in this chapter, is to teach you how to fight spiritually by using the sword of the spirit, which is the word of God. This was the great teaching God imparted in Joshua 1:8.

God does not want us, in these last days, to wait until we are attacked to fight, he wants us to be on the offense. The Lord instructed me that every day is a good day to attack and ambush the works of darkness. Satan and his demons do not take a break, so why should Christians? In this chapter, you will become a militant prayer warrior. Such people are desperately needed in our society. Will you volunteer and step up? Are you ready to be one of the ambush men of this generation? If so, then constantly practice with your sword in Jesus' name.

The Hebrew word for Ambush is "arab" meaning to lie in wait

The Merriam Webster defines Ambush as to attack someone or something by surprise.

The only thing Satan has going for himself is that he is consistent, therefore we must apply the same level of persistence by praying the word of God. We are fighting against spiritual forces that we cannot see, and that only the sword of the spirit can contend with. My prayer is that you will not be caught on the battlefield without being properly equipped with the word of God. As you use these scriptural prayer points in your prayer life, your ambush life will continue to be a success in Jesus' name. Amen.

"Because they met not the children of Israel with bread and with water, but hired Balaam against them, that he should curse them: howbeit our God turned the curse into a blessing." (Nehemiah 13:2)

Prayer point: "May every curse attached to my life, whether it be from my mother or my father's side, every generational curse that has travelled through my blood shall be turned into a blessing. In Jesus' name. Amen."

"Keep me, O Lord, from the hands of the wicked; preserve me from the violent man; who have purposed to overthrow my goings." (Psalm 140:4)

Prayer point: "Father God, may you overthrow any spirit or devils trying to overthrow my life, plans, career, ministry, children, or marriage. In Jesus' name. Amen."

"And it shall come to pass in that day, saith the Lord of hosts, [that] I will cut off the names of the idols out of the land, and they shall no more be remembered: and also, I will cause the prophets and the unclean spirit to pass out of the land." (Zechariah 13:2)

Prayer point: "Lord, I uproot and cut off by consuming fire, every unclean false prophet spirit coming into our churches. In Jesus' name. Amen."

"And the Lord said unto Joshua, fear them not: for I have delivered them into thine hand; there shall not a man of them stand before thee." (Joshua 10:8)

Prayer point: "This time, no witchcraft or demon, nor shall any failure, shame, disgrace, false friends, or evil people stand and challenge me. In Jesus' name. Amen."

"Therefore, [as] I live, saith the Lord God, I will prepare thee unto blood, and blood shall pursue thee: since thou hast not hated blood, even blood shall pursue thee." (Ezekiel 35:6)

Prayer point: "Father God, because the evil ones love to shed innocent blood, may the river of the blood of Jesus chase them down and drown them to their destruction. In Jesus' name. Amen."

"But the Lord [is] with me as a mighty terrible one: therefore, my persecutors shall stumble, and they shall not prevail: they shall be greatly ashamed; for they shall not prosper: [their] everlasting confusion shall never be forgotten." (Jeremiah 20:11)

Prayer point: "Lord, be with me like a mighty warrior. May the plans of the enemy stumble and not prevail or prosper. May everlasting shame be their portion. In Jesus' name. Amen."

"For a great door and effectual is opened unto me, and [there are] many adversaries." (1 Corinthians 16:9)

Prayer point: "Lord, may you send down flames of fire upon every enemy spirit standing in the way of my open door. In Jesus' name. Amen."

"And the watchmen of Saul in Gibeah of Benjamin looked; and, behold, the multitude melted away, and they went on beating down [one another]." (1 Samuel 14:16)

Prayer point: "Lord, may my enemies flee in fear and be turned against one another in total confusion. In Jesus' name. Amen."

"³And when Paul had gathered a bundle of sticks, and laid [them] on the fire, there came a viper out of the heat, and fastened on his hand. ⁴And when the barbarians saw the [venomous] beast hang on his hand, they said among themselves, No doubt this man is a murderer, whom, though he hath escaped the sea, yet vengeance suffereth not to live. ⁵And he shook off the beast into the fire, and felt no harm." (Acts 28:3-5)

Prayer point: "Lord, I shake every venomous demonic thing attached to my life into the fire. In Jesus' name. Amen."

"Pharaoh's chariots and his host hath he cast into the sea: his chosen captains also are drowned in the Red Sea." (Exodus 15:4)

Prayer point: "Father God, may you expose and drown in your spiritual Red Sea every person that has been attached to my life in an attempt to bring me back into bondage. In Jesus' name. Amen."

"And it came to pass, as he went into the house of one of the chief Pharisees to eat bread on the sabbath day, that they watched him." (Luke 14:1)

Prayer point: "Lord, may you pluck out or blind any demonic agent watching me anywhere, including my job, in my ministry, my children, my marriage, my money, or promotions. In Jesus' name. Amen."

"Let them be confounded that persecute me, but let not me be confounded: let them be dismayed, but let not me be dismayed: bring upon them the day of evil, and destroy them with double destruction." (Jeremiah 17:18)

Prayer point: "I decree double destruction upon all evil forces in my city that threaten my success. In Jesus name. Amen."

"But the Lord thy God shall deliver them unto thee, and shall destroy them with a mighty destruction, until they be destroyed." (Deuteronomy 7:23)

Prayer point: "Holy Spirit, may every satanic activity in our surroundings immediately become the victim of a mighty destruction. In Jesus' name. Amen."

"When the morning was come, the chief priests and elders of the people took counsel against Jesus to put him to death." (Matthew 27:1)

Prayer point: "Lord, may you disappoint the desire of every secret death meeting taking place against my life, as well as my children, my ministry, my pregnancy, my church family, and my pastor. In Jesus' name. Amen."

"Then went the Pharisees, and took counsel how they might entangle him in his talk." (Matthew 22:15)

Prayer point: "Lord, give me the wisdom to speak grace when I am before all people, especially when I am in the presence of those who hate me. In Jesus' name. Amen."

"[1]And he shewed me Joshua the high priest standing before the angel of the Lord, and Satan standing at his right hand to resist him. [2]And the Lord said unto Satan, The Lord rebuke thee, O Satan;" (Zechariah 3:1-2)

Prayer Point: "Father God, whoever has been placed in my life to condemn me, prosecute me, torment me with my past, or accuse me before you, I rebuke that self-righteous spirit in Jesus' name. Amen."

Printed in the United States
By Bookmasters